In the Spirit of Armorbearing

Small Group Study Edition

Taking Your Teams of Support to the Next Level

EARMA BROWN
INNER COURT PUBLISHING

In the Spirit of Armorbearing Small Group Study Edition

ISBN 978-0-9797701-1-1

Published in the United States of America

Legal Terms: This publication is designed to provide competent and reliable information regarding the subject matters covered. The author and publisher of this book and the accompanying materials have used their best efforts in preparing this book. The author and publisher make no representation or warranties with respect to the accuracy, applicability, fitness, or completeness of the contents of this book. They disclaim any warranties (expressed or implied), merchantability, or fitness for a particular purpose. The author and publisher shall in NO event be held liable for any loss or other damages, including but not limited to special, incidental, consequential, or other damages. The author and publisher do not warrant the performance, effectiveness or applicability of any sites listed in this book. All links are for informational purposes only and are not warranted for content, accuracy or any other implied or explicit purpose.

Editors: Marilyn Worsham, Felecia Opakgu
Cover Design: Jay Cookingham

DEDICATION

This book is dedicated to Pastors Mike and Kathy Hayes.

ACKNOWLEDGEMENTS

Thank you to Paul and Connie Brown for their seeds of support and encouragement to our ministry.

TABLE OF CONTENTS

INTRODUCTION

Dear Friend:

Over the years, as Varn and I ministered about armorbearing and the ministry of helps, people frequently asked us to define the ministry of an armorbearer or to help structure their armorbearer's team.

The *In the Spirit of Armorbearing Small Group Study Edition* answers those questions and more. It has taken us many years to learn these principles. The Holy Spirit, those He sent to impart to us, and hands-on experience have made them simple and easy to grasp.

Now I get the privilege of sharing those lessons with you in a workbook format. My desire is to communicate them to you in an easy and simple manner. Since, I am a teacher at heart; I hope you have as much fun as I did in putting this study guide together for you.

The workbook has been written with the goal of helping you to accomplish the task of fulfilling your call to effectively help God's leaders. In the following pages, I will present and challenge you to apply biblical armorbearing and ministry of helps principles to your life of service.

Utilizing the format of small group study you will follow a simple 5 step process:

- Read: a Lesson from a biblical character study.
- Consider: Thought provoking questions used to test and cement your knowledge of the helps principles.
- Remember: Detailed explanation of each principle to add further insight and add substance.
- Discuss: Questions to prompt discussion in a class or group setting.
- Act: with Practical, challenging assignments designed to put the principles into practice in your life.

You may use this workbook as your personal study guide. However since helps and armorbearing is all about working with people, the guide has been set up so that classes or groups may study together as well. Come on; let's get started in studying and applying God's principles of Helps.

Helping leaders and supporters in the local church,
Earma Brown

SMALL GROUP LEADER INSTRUCTIONS

Welcome Group Leader!

In her original book, *In the Spirit of Armorbearing*, author and Bible teacher *Earma Brown* explored principles of armorbearing and ministry of Helps. Now with the systematic and highly practical companion workbook, Earma personally coach you toward your highest potential as an armorbearer and servant leader teacher.

Utilizing the format of the small group or class you will follow a simple 5 step process:

1. Read a lesson from a biblical character study
2. Consider thought provoking questions used to test and cement your knowledge of the Helps principles
3. Remember detailed explanation of each principle to add further insight and add substance including memory principles.
4. Discuss questions to prompt discussion in class or group setting
5. Act with practical, challenging assignments designed to put the principles into practices in your life.

These teacher's tips for the *In the Spirit of Armorbearing Small Group Study Edition* have been designed specifically with you and your small group or class in mind. Training leaders and volunteers can be a challenge; we want to help you maximize your ability to impact the lives of others. These tips offer additional insight and how to approach teaching them to your class. In these tips you will find:

• *Goals* to keep in mind while teaching the Helps principles
• *Ways* to help people better understand and implement them
• A *suggested path* to guide the class during the discussion time
• A *goal for the Action Notes* section and additional ideas for helping your group to implement each principle

Your role as the teacher (leader) of a group is very important. We suggest that you familiarize yourself with all of the material in the study edition before presenting the information to your class. In addition to completing each section yourself, we suggest you look for ways to personalize the questions and activities to your particular group. Your role will be to:

• Make sure key concepts are understood
• Aid individual and group exercises
• Encourage and lead meaningful discussion
• Begin content application, and, most importantly,
• Establish a safe environment for learning and change to take place

Tips to Get Started

1. **Open your class or group to the congregation or if you are training select individuals to serve as armorbearers:**
   α. Choose the best people you can to take through the class.
   β. Pick people that are already volunteering faithfully. Yet be careful not to pull from someone else's most faithful volunteers.
2. **Make your class a safe place to learn:**
   α. Be open with your life and encourage open discussions.
   β. Respect the confidential information of others.
3. **Keep the right attitude:**
   α. As you progress in training people, remember it is a process for everyone. No one has developed to a great servant or leader over-night.
4. **Stay focused on your goal:**

α. The best teachers don't expect to get something back from the people they are investing in. They teach as mentors trying to help their students improve or gain more revelation. Training leaders and volunteers can be a challenge, but it will be rewarding.

Set Your Goals:

The goals of your class are to help your students understand how to:

• Define the term and ministry of an armorbearer
• Recognize and fulfill their call to the Ministry of Helps
• Gain a revelation of the anointing of God to serve
• Choose God's view of servanthood
• Understand the flow of God's authority
• Be the gift of support to God's leaders
• Develop the spirit of armorbearing right where you are

Ways to help them understand and implement helps principles:
• Give biblical examples.
• Offer personal examples as well.
• Teach God's way of helping.
• Validate their position of helps through biblical scripture.
• Be inclusive in your teaching; do your best to include all in your class.

Group Discussion:

Use the discussion starters to encourage the people in your group to open up and share after answering the questions. As your class time permits try to allow everyone the opportunity to express their answers. Your goal is to share your revelation of an armorbearer to get them to commit to serving in excellence in whatever capacity they are helping.

Assignment:

The goal of the Action Notes section is have your class connect with other armorbearers in effectiveness and success. Additionally, the exercise challenges the students to become doers of God's Word not just hearers. Once the exercise is completed, follow up with the group and have them share with the class the results of each particular exercise.

Additional Resources:

If you need additional resources for your personal study or your class, *Armorbearers International* is available to help. You may visit the companion website http://www.armorbearers.net for other materials, newsletters and the teaching ministry of Varn and Earma Brown.

May God's best blessings rest upon you, your family and ministry as you train armorbearers, leaders, ministry volunteers and support teams in the spirit and attitude of servanthood (armorbearing.)

Section I
Developing the Spirit
of Armorbearing

CHAPTER ONE

What is an Armorbearer?

Saul liked him very much and David became one of his armorbearers.
—1 Samuel 16:22b.

ℭℨ

In biblical days, an armorbearer was one who actually carried the shield and armor of his leader as he went into battle, often acting as his personal assistant. In our modern-day, I see no walking around fully suited in the classical armor of the early centuries.

Nevertheless, in the spiritual realm, we continue to need our armor and our armorbearers. Just as much as our early century counterparts, we in the ministry of service are to suit up in the Armor of the Spirit and carry the armor of God's leaders in the battle of faith.

A modern day armorbearer is one called by God to serve and help his assigned leader in life, ministry, and especially in the fight of faith.[4] In essence, an armorbearer is called to attend to, minister to, care for, help, be of use, assist, benefit, promote, support, make easy for, nourish, and encourage their leader.

Furthermore, God calls others to walk in the spirit of armorbearing. They may not be assigned specifically to one leader, but they possess the mindset and attitude of an armorbearer. The attitude of an armorbearer is one of servanthood. The mindset of an armorbearer, as well as those operating in the spirit of one, is to do what it takes to serve and support their leadership.[5]

Operating in the spirit of armorbearing can also be described as operating in the principles or pervading qualities of an armorbearer. The qualities that top the list are servanthood, commitment, attentiveness, support, help, loyalty, and faithfulness.

A Lesson from King David

King David offers the best example to pattern our armorbearing in the beginning. It was the first position in which David operated in King Saul's service.

In addition, he offers a good example of the qualifying spirit to gain if God has called you to operate in the spirit of an armorbearer. Some qualities that brought David before King Saul were:

- **Devotion.** God was able to qualify David because of his devotion to Him first. Secondly, he was obedient and faithful in the secret places. Is your devotion in the right order? Is God first, family, work, and then ministry?

- **Victorious.** David developed a victorious spirit by conquering each challenge as it came. He conquered the bear and lion before he faced the giant, Goliath. Remember your victories as you overcome challenges one day at a time.

- **Respect.** David was reverent and respectful of the ordained office of his leadership (king). Be an example; give respect to the God-ordained office you are serving.

- **Courage.** David counted the cost and took his place in service. Let us count the cost of our service and take our place.

God used these qualities to qualify David for his armorbearer's service to the king. We can use the same qualities in making sure we are qualified for the call of God on our lives.

Throughout this book and study guide we will examine other examples, some good, and others offering an example of what not to do. Sometimes it is just as expedient to know what not to do, as it is to realize what to do.[7]

Consider the Spirit of Armorbearing

Father God sets armorbearers in place. There is a call for His people to know and operate in the spirit of armorbearing and support throughout the Body of Christ.

Whether you are assigned as a personal armorbearer, or one God has designated to operate in the spirit of armorbearing toward your leaders, begin to consider the spirit of armorbearing: (review ITSOA ch. 1 pg. 3-9)

1. Define the term armorbearer in your own words:

_____

_____

_____

2. How would you define the spirit of armorbearing?

_____

_____

_____

3. What's the formal definition of serve?

_____

_____

_____

4. What principle mentioned in "Armorbearing Cultivated" did God warn us not to forget?

_____

_____

_____

5. What qualities qualified David for his service to King Saul as an armorbearer?

_____

_____

_____

Remember These Principles

The basic attitude of a modern day armorbearer is one of servanthood. Therefore, it's no surprise the general functions of an armorbearer: attend to, minister to, care for, help, be of use, assist, benefit, promote, support, make easy for, nourish and encourage are found in the formal definition of "serve".[8]

Whether you are assigned as a personal armorbearer, or one God has designated to operate in the spirit of armorbearing toward your leaders, remember to:

- **Attend to your leaders by supporting them in spirit and body.** If your leader is ministering, resolve to be there in support. The time is over for our excuses of "I was there with you in spirit." Let your support be in spirit and body.

- **Minister to them as your ministry.** See the support of your leaders as ministry. Remember, God does and so should we.

- **Care for them with God's compassion for His servants.** Be moved with God's compassion for your authorities. Your pastors and church leadership are people—and people need care.

- **Help, be of use, and assist them in the practical.** Be practical in your service. A past leader of mine would often instruct our team with, "Don't be so spiritual that you are no earthly good!"

- **Serve to their benefit.** Our society has become a self-centered world. Go against the natural flow; let your service be to the benefit of your leaders.

- **Promote them.** Be one of their biggest cheerleaders. Everyone needs encouragement. We all enjoy someone who is enthusiastically for us. Be that excited someone to your leadership.[6]

- **Give them the gift of support.** God has ordained a chain of support in ministry. He has called leaders and supporters. Be a part of that chain; link up with your leadership in support.

- **Be one that nourishes and encourages them.** To nourish is to refresh another. According to Webster's Dictionary, "refresh" means to make a person feel stronger, replenished, and stimulated or revived.[9]

Serve your leaders as one sent to make them stronger, replenished, and revived.

Discussion Starters

Answer the following questions for your personal study and/or discuss your answers when you meet with your armorbearer's class or study group.

1. Have you begun with the small of what God called you to do?

_____

_____

_____

2. What daily processes are you being faithful to in your position of service?

_____

_____

_____

3. What qualifies you for tomorrow's power in God?

_____

_____

_____

4. Examine your life; what small things have you been faithfully doing?

_____

_____

_____

5. God is always looking for someone willing to start with the small. Make a list of things that you started small in but have become larger. Choose one and share with the group.

_____

_____

_____

Action Notes

Interview or talk with someone you consider being a modern-day armorbearer. Locate someone that has served in an armorbearer's capacity. Ask that person the following questions:

1. When did you first realize you were called to be an armorbearer?

_____

_____

_____

2. What are some of the greatest challenges you found as an armorbearer?

_____

_____

_____

3. What contributed to your growth as an armorbearer?

_____

_____

_____

4. What is the best advice that you would give to someone who aspires to be an effective armorbearer?

_____

_____

_____

Next Chapter:

Are you called by God to serve? I believe God calls leaders and supporters. Read the next chapter for the details: *Fulfilling the High Call to Ministry.*

Memory Principle: Serve in the least

~~~~~~~~~~~~~~~~~~~~~~~~~~~~~~~~~~~~~

Whoever can be trusted with very little can also be trusted with much.
—Luke 16:10.

You don't have to be great to start, but you have to
start to be great. *—Keith Davis, Evangelist, NFL Football Player.*

CHAPTER TWO

Fulfilling Your High Call to Ministry

And God hath set some in the church, first apostles, secondarily prophets, thirdly teachers, after that miracles, then gifts of healing, helps, governments, diversities of tongues. —1 Corinthians 12:28 KJV.

 CୠB

The Body of Christ needs every office set in the Church by God even the one not mentioned as much called the ministry of helps. The ministry gifts such as apostles, prophets, evangelist, teachers, and pastors receive much acclaim and recognition, as it should be. The Body of Christ needs every office set in the Church by God. However, there is a ministry not mentioned as much also set in the Body by our Lord. That is the ministry of Helps.

A lesson from Prophet Elisha

Elisha, a businessman, was out plowing with twelve yoke of oxen when the call of God came to him. He changed his schedule and his life to accommodate the call of God. Moved and changed, he counted it all as nothing compared to answering God's call.

He accepted his call to the ministry of service without knowing the destiny awaiting him. God had already ordained Elisha as the next prophet of the land. There is no record that Elijah told Elisha what God said. After years of faithfully helping his leader, God promoted Elisha as one matured and prepared for the office of prophet.[3]

Elisha exemplified several responses to the call of God which we may pattern our service:

- **Immediacy.** He responded immediately.

- **Timeliness.** He organized his affairs: God, family, work, ministry and so on.

- **Attentiveness.** He heard God for himself. He did not go by what others said. Elijah even responded with, "That's between you and God." He followed and served him anyway.

- **Willingness.** He was willing to start with the small. There are few mentions of Elisha after his initial start with Elijah until the very end.

- **Obedience.** He did the details and ordinary tasks of serving his leader Elijah.

I believe there are more Elisha-spirited servants ready to answer the call. God desires more of us who will not be so concerned about our next promotion. He desires servants who are not saying, "O.K. God, I'll do this dish detail, but you better have something good waiting for me." Instead, there must be more of us who are saying, "Here am I, Lord."[3]

Consider the Call

Answering God's Call for Supporters

Through Scripture, we know God placed ministries in the church, not man.[9] A person should not enter the ministry just because someone told them they were suited for it. Let God call you and place you where He wills.[10] I encounter many who say, "I'm called to preach."

Yet they do not start with the small God puts before them to qualify them for their calling. When you are answering your call to serve, consider God may want you to spend a season in the ministry of helps before He matures you to your ministry office.

1. What two men in the New Testament started out as ministers of Helps but later became Evangelists?

_____

_____

_____

2. The Apostle Peter admonished us to be diligent with proving we really are called and chosen by the Lord. What eight virtues she list for us to work on developing?

_____

_____

_____

3. Of those eight virtues, which do you feel most developed in your life?

_____

_____

_____

4. Of those same eight virtues which are least developed in your life?

_____

_____

_____

5. Write 2 Timothy 2:21 below. How does it relate to your life of service?

_____

_____

_____

I have discovered that when I have felt like quitting the most, I did not know my high calling in this ministry of service. I began to realize that I did not help just because someone asked me. I serve and help because God called and chose me to be a minister of helps.[4] We are the called and chosen followers, now let us be faithful.[5]

There are some points to remember that will help us remain faithful to our high call to ministry:

- **Realize God set the ministry of helps in the Church.**[6] Perhaps you have been thinking that you just volunteer and God does not care about the details. Stop! He does. He designed a special place in His Church for the ministry of (details) helps.

- **Know that Jesus called and chose you.** In John 15:16, He said to us, "You did not choose me, but I chose you and appointed you to go and bear fruit-fruit that will last."[7]

- **Discover God looks upon the heart.** Many believe the ones who get the most attention from man are the most important. However, God sees the secret. King David set a principle like this in place in Israel that remains present today, noted in 1 Samuel 30:24, "The share of the man who stayed with the supplies is to be the same as that of him who went down to the battle. All will share alike."[8]

- **Choose to remain faithful.** Faithfulness continues to be a daily choice. Faithful people are faithful by choice. There are many promises that are yes and amen to the faithful of God.

- **Know that God rewards faithfulness.** He does not reward according to the office in which we serve, but according to the faithfulness shown. He is attentive to His faithful servants. He promises to show Himself faithful to the faithful ones.

Discussion Starters

Answer the following questions for your personal study and/or discuss your answers when you meet with your armorbearer's class or study group.

1. What ordinary tasks does God desire to do extraordinary things in your life?

_____

_____

_____

2. Have you ever overlooked the small, looking for the large?

_____

_____

_____

3. How are you proving you really are called and chosen by the Lord?

_____

_____

_____

4. Read 1 Corinthians 12:28. What gift do you think the armorbearer is a part of?

_____

_____

_____

5. When you hear the name Mother Teresa, write below your first thoughts?

_____

_____

_____

Action Notes

Research a person who appeared ordinary but accomplished extraordinary things for God? Name three things from that person's life that you would like to implement in yours:

1. _____

2. _____

3. _____

Next Chapter:

In the next chapter we cover *The Anointing to Serve*. Armorbearing is an administration of the ministry of helps. Our Father God has provided a divine endowment to serve effectively.

Memory Principle: Serve Using Your Abilities

~~~~~~

Take the talent from him and give it to the one who has ten talents.
—Matthew 25:28a

"Ideas won't keep; something must be done about them." *—Alfred North Whitehead.*

CHAPTER THREE

The Anointing to Serve

God has arranged the parts in the body every one of them, just as he wanted them to be. The eye cannot say to the hand, 'I don't need you!' And the head cannot say to the feet, 'I don't need you!' —1 Corinthians 12: 18a, 21 NIV.

ૹ

Have you ever thought of yourself as a gift to the body of Christ, specifically God's leaders? Realize your support means that much in God's plans. A short illustration of our sometimes-wrong thinking is: The eyes of the body said sarcastically to the ears, "We can do all the seeing around here. We don't really need you.

Besides, you are just a couple of ears. You sit all the way on the side of the head. Not in front like all eyes do." The ears responded, "I guess I'm not needed. Hair hides me most of the time. I suppose God just put me here on the side and forgot about me…" [9] Does that scenario sound like someone who has lost the value of his or her unique purpose?

In referring to the illustration above, the body would be handicapped without the function of the ears. Furthermore, it is not as if the eyes can effectively serve the purpose for which the ears are created. In the same way, we must realize no one can effectively fulfill our unique purpose given by God.

A Lesson from Two Deacons

Stephen and Phillip, two of the first deacons, demonstrated an anointing to serve. They started out waiting tables in the Apostles' feeding program. The Apostles qualified the first deacons with certain qualities that should be present in all who serve. At first glance, the Scripture only says that Stephen and Phillip were filled with the Spirit, wisdom, and faith.

After examination, I discovered that with these qualities alone, these men were fully equipped.[1] Look with me in the Book of Acts chapter 6 at what the Scripture says about these servants and their anointing.

In doing so, we will know what it requires to operate effectively in the anointing to serve:

- **Holy Spirit.** God chose Stephen and Phillip to serve, yet they walked in tremendous power and anointing of the Holy Ghost. To walk effectively in the anointing, we must allow the Holy Spirit to fill us; the same Holy Spirit that Jesus promised to send to help us, counsel us, and guide us in truth.[2] The Holy Spirit that empowers us to obey Christ will empower us to serve our Lord. An anointing from the Holy Spirit will evidence your service.[3]

- **Wisdom.** The apostle James instructed us, if a man were considered wise, it would be evidenced by his good life and by his actions done in humility. As he further explained wisdom, we can know that Stephen and Phillip served with a pure heart. They were peaceful, considerate of others, submitted to authority and merciful. They served wholeheartedly with sincerity and without selfish agendas.[4]

- **Faith.** Saul of Tarsus was still breathing out threats to the early Church at the time these servants of God came along. The largest portion of the New Testament Scripture had not yet been written, however Stephen and Phillip were full of faith. They exemplified their faith by what they did. Stephen was noted for his working of miracles among the people.

Phillip's faith exemplified his ability to follow the leading of the Holy Spirit. Jesus promised us that we could do the same marvelous acts of faith and even greater, "…anyone who has faith in Me will do what I have been doing. He will do even greater things than these, because I am going to the Father…You may ask Me for anything in My name, and I will do it." [5]

Just as any other ministry, it takes more than natural ability to effectively fulfill the ministry of serving. It takes an anointing (a supernatural enablement) from the Holy Spirit. We may pattern our service after men full of the Holy Spirit, wisdom, and faith walking in the anointing of the Lord.

Consider the Anointing

Developing Your Service as a Gift to Others

Armorbearing is an administration of the ministry of helps. Our heavenly Father has provided an anointing to serve, a divine endowment to serve effectively. God's gifts and callings are with out repentance, but the anointing may decrease and fade. [6] I compare the anointing with the talents Jesus spoke of in His parable of the talents. [7]

The master gave one man a level one measure of anointing. Another received a level two anointing. Yet, another was given a level five anointing, each according to his ability. Two of them used what he gave them and it multiplied. The one that received the level one anointing did not use his anointing and suffered great loss.

1. How do you monitor your zeal? What steps have you taken to keep your anointing and zeal hot?

_____

_____

2. Do you have a current Bible study or reading plan? If so, describe it below.

_____

_____

3. Do you fast? If so, how often do you fast?

_____

_____

4. What did the Apostle Paul mean when he said, "The gifts are useless in your life if you don't have love?

_____

_____

5. The author made the statement, "Prayer prepares you for anointed service." If you agree, how has prayer prepared you for anointed service?

_____

_____

Remember These Principles

Most people think of the anointing as something mystical that either you have or do not have. On the other hand, many mistakenly think God's power to do only rests upon those who publicly minister-preach, teach, prophesy, etc.

I have heard it often said of someone, "He's not anointed to do anything. He has no ministry." Yet, when I see this person operating in their gifts of administration, I see the anointing. When I observe them doing the work of the ministry of helps, I recognize the anointing to serve.

God's anointing empowers you to do whatever He calls you to do. If the Holy Spirit has gifted you to serve, begin to recognize the anointing. Know that you have the anointing and equipment to do all that God created you to be and do. The anointing will:

• Empower you to discern what needs to be done

- Empower you to do the practical

- Empower you to do the unlikely

- Empower you to give the word of encouragement

- Empower you to nourish

- Empower you to anticipate needs

- Empower you to go the extra mile

Know that wherever God has called you to serve, He has provided a supernatural enablement to accomplish His work.

Discussion Starters

Answer the following questions for your personal study and/or discuss your answers when you meet with your armorbearer s class or study group.

1. Have you realized you are developing your anointing through the details of service? If so, what details of service do you think God is using in your life?

_____

_____

_____

2. What has God empowered you to do through His anointing?

_____

_____

_____

3. The author said, God led me to protect my anointing. What has God led you to do to protect the anointing in your life?

_____

_____

_____

4. Describe below Stephen and Phillips work in the Ministry of Helps.

_____

_____

_____

5. What patterns do you see in Stephen and Phillip s life that we may implement in our modern-day life?

_____

_____

_____

Action Notes

The author used the following biblical text for the *Anointed to Serve* chapter. *1 Corinthian 12: 4-7 Now there are varieties of gifts, but the same Spirit. And there are varieties of ministries, and the same Lord. And there are varieties of administrations, but the same God, who works all things in all persons. But to each one is given the manifestation of the Spirit for the common good.*

Study these and pretend a friend came to you and asked you to explain them in your own words. Write briefly would you would say below.

_____

_____

_____

_____

_____

_____

Ready for *Chapter Four: Choosing God's View of Servanthood*? Servanthood is an attitude for the entire Church in which each gift and ministry must seek to continue. This lesson will reveal how we really feel...

Memory Principle: Serve with All Your Might

~~~~~~

Whatever your hands find to do, do it with all your might. —Ecclesiastes 9:10a

"Whatever you are, be a good one." *—Abraham Lincoln.*

CHAPTER FOUR

Choosing God's View of Servanthood

*Having gifts (faculties, talents, qualities) that differ according to the grace given us,
let us use them: He, whose gift is practical service, let him give himself to serving.*
—Romans 12:6-7 AMP

ℭ

S ervanthood is an attitude. It is an attitude that God esteems highly. In the Body of Christ, Jesus is our chief example, He not counting Himself equal with God, took on the very nature of a servant. How much more should we the Body of Christ do the same? Servanthood is an attitude for the entire Church in which each gift and ministry must seek to continue.

A Lesson from a Family of Gatekeepers

According to the writer of I Chronicles, those chosen to serve as gatekeepers of the House of God were selected based on their genealogies, family of Levites, and because of their reliability.[3] Their appointed positions of trust continue to give us insight to what God requires in His New Covenant servants. They exemplified simple qualities that are relevant to our service today:

- **Faithfulness.** The Lord is faithful to the faithful. Did your ancestors serve God? If so, carry the torch in your generation. If not, start a record of faithfulness to God in your family. In earlier times, Phinehas, son of Eleazar, was in charge of the gatekeepers, and the Lord was with him.[4]

- **Reliability.** We know that we can rely and depend on God. However, can He depend and rely on our service in His modern day House (Church)? They were chosen from their villages on the basis of their genealogies, and they were appointed by David and the prophet Samuel because of their reliability.[5]

- **Trustworthiness.** One of the definitions of trust is 'responsibility resulting from confidence placed in one.' God has trusted us with His gifts and calling. We are responsible (like it or not) for what we do with them. Are we trustworthy of the confidence He has placed in us? The four head gatekeepers, all Levites, were in an office of great trust, for they were responsible for the rooms and treasuries in the house of God.[6]

- **Responsibility.** If you are parents of teenagers, you often have to judge if your children are responsible enough to handle certain tasks. Our Father God is the same about us as His children. He will check to see how responsible we are with the small things of the Kingdom before He gives us the weighty tasks. Know that how you handle the anointing you have now, will determine the level of anointing you will operate in tomorrow. Others were responsible for the furniture, the items in the sanctuary, and the supplies such as fine flour, wine, incense and spices.[7]

- **Focus.** In our busy lives, it can be difficult to stay focused. It is easy to lose sight of what should be the center of our attention. I have at different times, become too busy in the Lord. Each time to regain my focus, I would go to the Lord to determine what He called me to do and what I agreed to do because it sounded good at the time. Graciously, He would point to His best for me. Let God's best for you be your focus. The cantors, free from other responsibilities were all prominent Levites. They lived in Jerusalem at the house of

God and were on duty at all hours.[8]

Consider Servant-hood

Becoming a true servant of God

Servanthood is an attitude for the entire Church in which each gift and ministry must seek to continue. This lesson will reveal how we really feel. Remembering why we do what we do will keep us motivated to remain faithful and serving for the right reason. Re-examine why you do what you do. Discover afresh, Jesus is the best reason for serving. Then go ahead serve your best because you love Jesus. But first answer these questions about servanthood:

1. What was your last random act of kindness?

_____

_____

_____

2. In your own words, what did the Apostle Paul mean when he said, "Serve wholeheartedly as if you were serving the Lord, not men. Eph. 6:7

_____

_____

_____

3. Why do you serve as an armorbearer, assistant, helper, or volunteer?

_____

_____

4. Is there someone serving you in any capacity that you should know better? Write names of 3 people and 2 things you know about them: (i.e. janitor, cook, security, usher, and greeter)

_____

_____

_____

5. Have you spiraled into the negative thinking, "No one appreciates me? No one even said thank you…, lately?" If so, how did you change your thinking?

_____

_____

_____

Remember these principles

What is your perspective on servanthood? When you think of servanthood, do you envision it as an activity performed by relatively low-skilled people at the bottom of the positional ladder? Servanthood is not a position it is an attitude.

People who have humility can easily be recognized, as well as those without this attitude. We have all encountered a rude waiter in a restaurant, or a utility company employee who does not want to be bothered. The cashier on the phone talking to a friend, instead of helping you is a classic.

But wait; let's stop by the Church before we complete the illustration of this point. Have you met an unfriendly greeter? Or perhaps the usher who prods and pushes the sheep into place has prodded you. Then there is the Church employee who has forgotten that they took their job as an opportunity to minister. So what are the qualities that make a person with a serving attitude so easily recognizable?

- They allow God to purify their motives

- They put others ahead of their own agenda

- They possess the confidence to serve

- They initiate service to others

- They are not position conscious

- They serve with love and compassion for God's people

All can easily recognize those that are truly servant-hearted. Are you recognized often as a servant-hearted person?

Discussion Starters

Answer the following questions for your personal study and/or discuss your answers when you meet with your armorbearer s class or study group.

1. Is your servanthood an attitude?

_____

_____

_____

2. What season are you in as the chosen of God? If you can identify your season describe it below.

_____

_____

_____

3. Are you preparing your service to God as a torch to pass to the next generation? If so, write how you are doing this below.

_____

_____

_____

4. The qualities the author listed in the Pattern Your Service pg. 26-27 section are: faithfulness, reliability, trustworthiness, responsibility, focus. How are they relevant to you as an armorbearer?

_____

_____

_____

5. What gifts of helps have you been entrusted with by God?

_____

_____

_____

Action Notes

Step out of your comfort zone. Strive to serve in those capacities that challenge you, stretch you, and make you grow. Serve even if it makes you uncomfortable for a season. Surprise a few people close to you by doing something for them they would not ordinarily expect from you. For this exercise, as your action step find someone who needs your serving attitude and perform a random act of kindness for them. After doing so, describe briefly below your experience and their reaction.

_____

_____

_____

_____

We pray a special blessing over you and your ministry as God's servant. Next chapter, we discuss *Understanding the Flow of Authority: Accountability acts as a Safeguard in Our Lives*. Are you flowing in authority? All day long if we are wise, we flow in and under authority. There is a God given measure of rule over every area of life.

Memory Principle: Serve with a Willing Spirit

~~~~~~

If you are willing and obedient you will eat the good of the land —Isaiah 1:19.

"Nothing is impossible to a willing heart." —*Unknown*.

CHAPTER FIVE

Understanding the Flow of Authority

Everyone must submit himself to the governing authorities, for there is no authority except that which God has established. The authorities that exist have been established by God. —Romans 13:1

☙

S cripture establishes God has given all authority. There is also a God-given measure of rule, an area, or sphere of ruler ship. We can see this authority principle in our homes, neighborhoods, counties, cities, states, and the nations.

There is an authority figure or figures set over each area. Even Satan has implemented this powerful principle in his kingdom of authorities and rulers in the dark world. All day long, if we are wise, we flow in and under authority.

A Lesson from the Centurion

The centurion, whose servant was sick, applied this authority flow to his faith in Jesus. According to the gospel of Matthew, when the centurion heard that Jesus was in town, he went to Him asking for help. "Lord," he said, "My servant lies at home paralyzed and in terrible suffering."

Jesus was ready to go and heal the servant, but the centurion stopped him saying, "…just say the word, and my servant will be healed. For I myself am a man under authority, with soldiers under me. I tell this one, 'Go.' And he goes; and that one, 'Come' and he comes. I say to my servant, 'Do this,' and he does it." Jesus commended the centurion's faith and understanding of authority.

Matthew records that the centurion's servant was healed at the same hour he asked. The centurion offers us a simple pattern of understanding the flow of authority instituted by God.[3]

Consider the Flow of Authority

Accountability is a Safeguard in Our Lives

Are you flowing in authority? All day long if we are wise, we flow in and under authority. There is a God given measure of rule over every area of life. By submitting to authority in our life, we become accountable. In fact, where we see submit, it can be interchanged with be accountable. (Review ITSOA ch. 5, pg. 36-37)

1. The author sates submit and be accountable can be interchanged, how so?

_____

_____

_____

2. Define accountability?

_____

_____

_____

3. According to the author, "Mentorship will keep the doors of accountability open." In your own words, explain below what else promotes accountability.

_____

_____

_____

4. Why do you think the author declares God wants renewed respect for His authority structure?

_____

_____

_____

5. Write out the words of Scripture 1 Timothy 2:1, 2 below and do it today.

_____

_____

_____

We must be willing to apply this principle of authority to the authority God has set in our lives. It may be parental authority, church authority, school authority, work or governmental authority. No one is exempt from being under authority and accountable to an authority in his or her life.

In addition, no one remains accountable to authority by accident. It requires a decision. Webster's dictionary tells us *accountable* means: being responsible, liable, or explainable.

All levels of our life and relationships need accountability. Even so, not many people truly enjoy being accountable. We don't always enjoy questions like: Where were you last night? Where were you on Sunday morning? Why did you handle it like that? Is there any money left in the account? Our flesh (human nature) enjoys being question-free about what it is doing or not doing.

Those in authority hold us accountable in our lives. Parents hold their children accountable, spouses hold each other accountable, and employers hold their employees' accountable, governing agencies hold employers accountable, and so on. We, the family of God, hold each other accountable in Christ. Father God holds us all accountable.

Discussion Starters

Answer the following questions for your personal study and/or discuss your answers when you meet with your armorbearer s class or study group.

1. Are you a leader? Describe how you flow in and under authority in your life.

_____

_____

_____

2. Name three people to whom you are accountable.

_____

_____

_____

3. How similar are you to the centurion? Describe any similarities.

_____

_____

_____

4. According to Romans 13:1 which authorities are established by God and which are not?

_____

_____

_____

5. Name three people that are accountable to you?

_____

_____

_____

Action Notes

Consider one person which is accountable to you and write three things you wish they would do that would improve their ability to flow under your authority. (i.e. follow my instructions exactly, be on time, etc.)

Then consider one person to whom you are accountable and name three things that you could do to flow under their authority more effectively.

_____

_____

_____

_____

_____

_____

God bless you in your ministry of armorbearing. Anticipating the next chapter? In chapter six, we discuss *Developing the Gift of Support: Your Gift is a Part of God's Plan.* Is your support a gift? God, in His mercy, designed a gift of support for His leaders still active today.

Visit us again on the web http://www.armorbearers.net for insightful free articles of encouragement for you or visit our new Bible study form and get other teaching on this and other helps principles!

Memory Principle: Serve Conquering Oneself

~~~~~~

Like a boxer I buffet my body--handle it roughly, discipline it and subdue it.
—1 Corinthians 9:27a.

"The hardest victory is victory over self." —Aristotle.

CHAPTER SIX

Developing the Gift of Support

But bring your brothers, the tribe of Levi, to join you and serve you while you and your sons minister before the Tent of the Testimony. They are to serve you and take care of the details of the Tent. I myself have selected your fellow Levites from among the Israelites as a gift to you, dedicated to the Lord to take care of the details at the Tent of Meeting. —Numbers 18:2, 3, 6 paraphrased.

CB

I n the Old Testament, God gave the Levites' help as a gift to Aaron and his sons. It was not earned for Aaron was not any more deserving than we are of God's gifts to us. God, in His mercy, designed a chain of support still active today. He literally called out the Levites solely as a support ministry to the priesthood and offered them to Aaron and his sons as a gift.[2]

A Lesson from the Levite Brothers

God's design and purpose for our Levite brothers reflect a beautiful pattern for his New Testament servants today. God set the Levites apart and their practical ministry offered as a gift. I myself have selected your fellow Levites from among the Israelites as a gift to you, dedicated to the Lord to take care of the details at the Tent of Meeting. -Num. 18:6

They were to help the men of God and take care of all the details of the Tent. Look with me at some simple principles set forth that will under gird and still apply to our modern day support ministries:

God appointed the Levites. He selected the Levite brothers from among the other Israelites to join Aaron and his sons in service. In a similar fashion, the writer of the first book of Corinthians tells us, "God chooses and puts His saints exactly where he wants them in the Body of Christ. 3 I believe it is worth injecting, if we allow him.

The Lord dedicated the Levites to Himself. One of the meanings given for dedication as well as holy is 'set apart'. Interchanging the words we could say, "The Levites were set apart for the Lord." The Apostle Peter reminds us of an Old Testament command that still applies to God's servants today saying, "Be holy as I am holy." 4 Join me as I ask myself, "How set apart am I to the Lord for service in His Church?"

God gave the Levites' ministry as a gift. What a wonderful honor given to the Levite tribe of Israel. When I prepare a gift for my child, I make sure it is the best quality that I can find. The physician Luke phrased it in a similar way referring to God's gifts saying, "If your nature is evil and you know how to give good gifts to your children, how much more will your Father in heaven give a good gift." 5 The helps ministry is a gift to our ministry leaders in the Church. Let us endeavor to walk worthy of this calling.

God assigned the Levites to the details of the Tent. They were given duties concerning the Tent while the priest ministered before the Lord. Perhaps the early Church apostles had this fact in mind when they assigned the first seven to handle the details of ministry while they spent more time before the Lord in prayer and the ministry of the word. Have you been assigned the details of the ministry while your leadership ministers before the Lord? If so, know that you have been given a great honor.

Consider the Gift of Support

Your gift of support is a part of God's plan

Is your support a gift? God, in His mercy, designed a gift of support for His leaders still active today. Have you ever thought of yourself as a gift to the Body of Christ, specifically God's leaders? Realize your support means that much in God's plans for His Church. (pg. 42, 43)

1. To strengthen right perspective of your service and gift, the author list four points to include in your thinking, what are they?

_____

_____

_____

2. According to 1 Corinthian 12:12-21 which parts of the body may function alone?

_____

_____

_____

3. Who assigned the Levites to help Aaron and his sons?

_____

_____

_____

4. One of the meanings given for dedication as well as holy is

_____

_____

_____

5. God appointed the Levites to the details of the Tent. How may they relate to the modern day ministries of the Church?

_____

_____

_____

Remember These Principles

God presented the support ministries to His people as a gift. Through the writer of Exodus, it was revealed that Aaron was called to support Moses.6 Now it's clear that the Levites were called to support Aaron. In the New Testament, we see an example in the first deacons of the church, men called to serve the people; especially widows and orphans while, the Apostles prayed and ministered the Word.

God has designed a chain of support. Look at God's chain of support in the Old Testament versus our local Church body:

- God called Moses to lead the Israelites

- God called Senior Pastors to lead Church Body

- God called Aaron to be Moses' helper and associate priest God called pastoral staff to assist Senior Pastors

- God called Levites to minister to priesthood God called helps ministry to help ministry leaders

- God called Israelites to support priest & Levites God called congregation to support leadership team

We need each other in God's chain of support. We must begin to take our place and serve as a strong link in God's chain. As an example look again to the book of Exodus, the Israelites were in a battle with the Amalekites.[7]

Moses went to the top of a mountain and held the staff out over the battle. As long as his arms were up, the Israelites prevailed. However, when his hands were down, the Amalekites were winning. Aaron and Hur put a large rock under Moses for him to sit on. Then one stood on each side to hold his arms up in the air.

God could have supernaturally strengthened Moses' arms to the point where he did not need Aaron and Hur to hold them up. I believe God wanted to spotlight our need for each other, especially in times of battle. Pastor Gordon Banks phrased it like this, "Working alone in Jesus, you may eventually win. But working together in Jesus, you win quickly."

Often without support, our personal battles are longer than necessary. In addition, if we do not allow others to share in our battle, we cheat them of their share in the joy of victory. Jesus spoke of this when He said, "Those that share in My sufferings, I will share My glory with them." [8]

Discussion Starters

Answer the following questions for your personal study and/or discuss your answers when you meet with your armorbearer s class or study group.

1. Are you a link in God s chain of support?

_____

_____

_____

2. How can you make your connection with others stronger in His system of support?

_____

_____

_____

3. Is your service a gift to the Body of Christ; if not what can you do to make it so?

_____

_____

_____

4. Write the words of Scripture Numbers 18:2, 3, and 6 below. In your opinion, how do these scriptures relate to being an armorbearer?

_____

_____

_____

5. Describe the chain of support in your church?

_____

_____

_____

Action Notes

Developing strong chains of support includes building strong and stronger relationships with your team or group. For this action exercise, spend time developing relationship with someone that you need to know better on your team.

Look for an appropriate time to talk with them about something outside of your service together. (i.e. go to lunch, breakfast, etc.) If that is not an option, just begin a conversation about their family, work, hobbies, etc. Make it a goal to learn three things about that person on your team. Write what you have learned below.

_____

_____

_____

_____

_____

_____

_____

_____

_____

May God continue to bless you with His wisdom. Keep going to the final chapter of this section: Seven – *Developing the Spirit of Armorbearing: Serving God with His principles*. In any administration of the helps ministry, one may operate in the spirit of armorbearing. We review a list of biblical characters to pattern our service.

Memory Principle: Serve Giving Support

~~~~~~

When Moses' hands grew tired, they took a stone and put it under him and he sat on it. Aaron and Hur held his hands up--one on one side, one on the other--so that his hands remained steady until sunset." —Exodus 17:12

"Give the Church your gift of support." —*Earma Brown.*

CHAPTER SEVEN

Developing the Spirit of Armorbearing

And I will come down and talk with thee there: and I will take of the spirit which is upon thee, and will put it upon them: and thy shall bear the burden of the people with thee, that thou bear it not thy alone.—Numbers 11:17

୯୪

In any administration of the helps ministry, one may operate in the spirit of armorbearing. In a simile, I gathered a succession of biblical characters, each displaying a pervading quality of armorbearing. In chapters one through six, we have examined David's qualifying attitude, Elisha's answer to God's call and his devotion and Stephen and Phillip's humility and power with God.

We introduced the Israelite gatekeepers' trusted responsibilities, the centurion's understanding of authority and the Levites gift of support. We may pattern our service from this list of biblical characters and their qualities.

A Lesson from Prophet Jeremiah's Assistant

There is a young man that especially exemplified the spirit of armorbearing in his actions. His name was Baruch, assistant to Prophet Jeremiah. Prophet Jeremiah and Baruch lived during a time that God was judging His people for their continued disobedience.

The times were evil and many times Jeremiah was thrown in jail for the message from God he was compelled to give. From jail, he continued to dictate God's Words to his assistant Baruch.

Baruch, following Jeremiah's instructions would go to the temple and read the Word of God to the people. Even though Baruch, a human like us, grew weary with all the accusations and persecutions that came along with serving one of God's leaders, he remained faithful. God sent him a word of encouragement to remain thankful for his life.

For in the midst of all the trouble He was sending upon his chosen nation He promised to protect him wherever he went as a reward. Baruch offers us a model of courage, obedience, and faithfulness in serving God's leader.1

Consider the Spirit of Armorbearing

Serving God through his principles

In any administration of the helps ministry, one may operate in the spirit of armor bearing. We review a list of biblical characters to pattern our service. In refining silver or gold, the metal is put through intense heat, more than several times to remove dross and impurities. Each time, the gold or silver comes out improved, more clear, and precise. There are ways to refine the spirit of armorbearing.

1. What parable did Jesus tell which demonstrated our need to volunteer?

_____

_____

_____

2. According to Scripture Jesus will come again. According to John 9:4 why must we serve with a sense of urgency?

_____

_____

_____

3. Jesus is our chief example. What was he teaching us through demonstration in John 15:13?

_____

_____

_____

4. The lack of what virtue may lead to rebelling against authority? (pg. 49)

_____

_____

_____

5. Our enemy, the devil, knows the importance of people fulfilling their call to help and support God's leaders. Therefore he does what? (pg. 49)

_____

_____

_____

Remember these Principles

In the first chapter, armorbearer was traced to the Hebrew word *nasa*, meaning to support or simply help. With this in mind, anyone may operate in the spirit of helping someone in leadership. No title is needed to lift up the arms of God's leaders. Perhaps you are one of those God has called from the pew to simply start where you are, helping your leadership. As one operating in the spirit of armorbearing, remember to develop the qualities found in servanthood:

- **Be attentive.** Watch for and observe your leaders' needs. Most may be in the mindset that all is taken care of in the Church. However, if you look with a discerning eye, God will lead you where to lend a hand.

- **Minister to your leadership.** Treat your service as ministry. God will show you where you are needed most. Remember He puts each person just where He wants him or her to be.[2]

- **Care for God's servants.** Flow in His compassion for your leaders. Take on the advice of the apostle Peter, "And now this word to all of you: You should be like one big happy family, full of compassion for each other, loving one another with tender hearts and humble minds." [3]

- **Assist your leaders in the practical.** The helps ministry is a practical ministry. God inspires our authorities with a great plan or vision but they need your help with the details.

- **Serve to their benefit.** God calls us men pleasers if we serve only to impress others. Examine your service. Is it to your leaders' benefit or to your benefit only?

- **Empower your leaders.** In a self-centered society, it can be difficult to find people who are willing to lay aside their needs to attend to another. The writer of John instructs with, "Greater love has no one than this that he lay down his life for his friend." [4] You can do it, lay self aside, and promote another. As you do so, God will certainly empower you and promote you in due season.

- **Be the gift of support to them.** Acknowledge God has set you in place to support your leaders. Know that you come highly recommended by the Father. You are the gift of support.

- **Nourish and encourage your leadership team.** Do not always get in the receiving line. Mature and know that God is your ultimate source. Be prepared for God to use you to offer nourishment and encouragement to your leaders.

Discussion Starters

Answer the following questions for your personal study and/or discuss your answers when you meet with your armorbearer's class or study group.

1. Are you called by God to operate in the spirit of armorbearing to your leadership? If so, how are you doing so?

_____

_____

_____

2. Would your reputation in the ministry of serving identify you for greater service in God?

_____

_____

_____

3. Do you have a sense of urgency in your service to God?

_____

_____

_____

4. What qualities from Prophet Jeremiah s assistant Baruch should we model?

_____

_____

_____

5. Lack of continued submission to authority may be one of the biggest causes of turnover among the ranks of God s army. Describe your opinion of this statement below:

_____

_____

_____

Action Notes

You and each person on your armorbearer's or ministry of helps team have a unique set of gifts, talents, training and experiences. For this exercise, if not already, take a gift assessment test such as *Discover Your God Given Gifts* by *Don & Katie Fortune*.

Then have each person, including yourself, fill out the mini-survey below. Individually review each person's test and survey answers and discuss with him or her the role he or she plays on the team. Also, direct the team to opportunities that are available to them to improve or simply use their skills.

1. What job task do you enjoy doing the most? Why?

_____

_____

_____

2. What job or task do you least enjoy? Why?

_____

_____

_____

3. What are your hobbies and interest?

_____

_____

_____

4. What is your vocational or formal training? (degrees, certifications, classes taken)

_____

_____

_____

5. Outside of your obvious job skills, what other skills or training do you have?

_____

_____

_____

6. In what area do you think you would best serve the team?

_____

_____

_____

7. What are your career goals?

_____

_____

_____

8. How do you benefit from being a member of this team?

_____

_____

_____

9. How does the team benefit from having you as a member?

_____

_____

_____

Next Chapter:

May God bless and prosper you in your ministry of armorbearing right where you are. Read the next chapter *The Ministry of Details*. Everyone loves it when someone shows they care. Show your Pastors and leaders you care with attention to the details.

Memory Principle: Serve in Harmony

~~~~~~

If I speak in the tongues of men and of angels, but have not love. I am only a resounding going or a clanging cymbal. —1 Corinthians 13:1

"Hatred paralyzes life; love releases it. Hatred confuses life; love harmonizes it. Hatred darkens life; love illumines it." —*Dr. Martin L. King, Jr.*

CHAPTER EIGHT

The Ministry of Details

And God hath set some in the church, first apostles, secondarily prophets, thirdly teachers, after that miracles, then gifts of healings, helps, governments, diversities of tongues. —1 Corinthians 12:28 KJV

ॐ

Agnes Gonzha Bojaxhiu, better known as, Mother Teresa, said, "I accept in the name of the poor," when she was awarded the 1979 Nobel Peace Prize. Before representing the poor, *Mother Teresa,* a teacher and then a principal, received a "call within a call" during a train ride, in which she felt God directing her to the slums.

By the end of her life, she and more than 3,000 sisters, who followed her, were operating a worldwide network of some 350 missions. A fellow nun said about her, "Mother is very ordinary. When people meet her, she surprises them with her ordinariness. But she allows God to work through her, and He has done extraordinary things." God deliberately chooses what we consider ordinary, even foolish, to confound the wise of our world.

Speaking of ordinary, how would the church manage without the hands that help with the details? When something practical needs to be done, a person anointed to help steps in and sees to it that the job is completed. God is practical and good and so are they that help. The behind-the-scene jobs in the church often go unrecognized. Yet the humble tasks are the ones we benefit from the most.

There are faithful people who maintain the grounds, clean our church, make repairs, do plumbing, assist with the administration, type bulletins, usher, greet, watch babies, make sure the sound and electronics work smoothly, make snacks and food for the church, do dishes or simply help with the details. Praise God for those serving in the ministry of helps.

Through Scripture, we know God placed ministries in the church, not man. A person should not enter the ministry just because someone told them they were suited for it. Let God call you and place you where He wills. I encounter many who say, "I'm called to preach." Yet they do not start with the small God puts before them to qualify them for their calling. When you are answering your call to serve, consider God may want you to spend a season in the ministry of helps before He matures you to your ministry office.

Remember Stephen and Phillip, who started in the ministry of helps but later operated as evangelists? They were faithful to help where God assigned them first. Also, I must mention that there were five others assigned to help. There are no other references of them in the Bible. I believe they continued faithfully serving in the ministry of helps.

If you are uncertain of your call to the ministry of helps, ask God to confirm your calling. Apostle Peter admonishes us to be diligent with proving that we really are called and chosen by the Lord. Give all diligence to exercising and developing His virtues the fruit of the Spirit (listed below), so that you may be effective and productive in your gifts and calling:

Faith. Exercise your faith at every opportunity. Faith pleases God. Everyone receives a measure of faith to function within whatever gift God has graced him. He whose gift is practical service, let him give himself to serving according to the proportion of his faith.

Virtue. After exercising your faith, develop virtue, which is spiritual excellence. Daniel, in serving God and exercising his faith, developed an excellent spirit. So much so that he and his fellow Jewish slaves were found ten times better in all respects than the others assigned to the Kings' service.

Knowledge. In developing an excellent spirit, add knowledge. Get to know your Heavenly Father. As we know Him better, we are sure to discover our destiny and what He wants us to do   step by step.

Paul wrote to the saints in Ephesus, "I keep asking that the God of our Lord Jesus Christ, the glorious Father, may give you the Spirit of wisdom and revelation, so that you may know Him better."

Self-control. In exercising knowledge, develop self-control. We live in a world of steadily decreasing self-control. The number of road rage incidents is evidence to that. More than half of U.S. Adults are over-weight.

Many suffer from lack of control in eating habits. Drug abuse and overdose have increased beyond what our ancestors would recognize. In gaining self-control, more and more we learn to put aside our own desires so that we may fulfill God's desires.

Patience. When allowing the Holy Spirit to help you gain more self-control, add patience. I overheard a teacher's advice to his student, "Never pray for patience, because you will get lots of problems with opportunity to learn patience." The student's reply was, "I don't believe that God would send me problems to teach me anything."

Look in on what the Apostle Paul writes the Roman Christians, "We can rejoice, too, when we run into problems and trials, for we know that they are good for us—they help us learn to be patient. And patience develops strength of character in us and helps us trust God more each time we use it, until finally our hope and faith are strong and steady." What do you think of the teacher's advice?

Godliness. As you develop patience, put aside your own desires in an increasing measure, so that God may have His way with you in godliness. The Apostle Peter wrote the Jewish Christians and now us, "Obey God, because you are His children; don't slip back into your old ways—doing evil because you knew no better.

However, be holy now in everything you do, just as the Lord is holy, who invited you to be His child. He Himself said, 'You must be holy, for I am holy.'"

Brotherly affection. When practicing godliness, develop brotherly affection. Love one another with brotherly affection—as members of one family—giving precedence and showing honor to one another. Love the brotherhood of believers. Pray for God's people with strong purpose.

As you pray for the Body of Christ, interceding on their behalf, your concern will become Christ's compassion. Your hands and feet will become Christ's members, reaching out to the saints. Your affection will become Christ's love flowing through you for His Church.

Love. When praying for the church in brotherly affection, finally add love. Let love guide your speech and actions. In my B.C. before Christ days, I would often hurt others by just bluntly telling them the truth. If anyone would say anything to me about it, I would respond with, "Well, it was the truth!"

After meeting Christ, I continued with this speaking the truth. But each time I did, I would feel so miserable, I was compelled to apologize. Later, after prayer, the Holy Spirit instructed me I could speak the truth, but in love. I discovered that truth in love is often silent.

Let love guide your actions. The Apostle John wrote to his friends in the faith, "Little children, let us stop just saying we love people; let us really love them, and show it by our actions." Let love guide your life. Grow to love more and more.

The more we add and develop these qualities in our life, the more useful and fruitful we will be to our Master, Lord Jesus. We will become the special vessels prepared and ready for the Master's use.

In Paul's second letter to Timothy, he encourages us to be like the expensive dishes in God's house, "If you stay away from sin, you will be like one of these dishes made of purest gold—the very best in the house—so that Christ Himself can use you for His highest purposes."

Next Chapter

Are you ready for the next section containing additional insight for your personal study or your small group study? We have compiled this section of the book especially for those called to become an armorbearer or lead other armorbearers into service. Don't stop reading now. *Serving God's Leader as*

Armorbearer contains important teaching about armorbearing and God's leaders.

Memory Principle: Serve Until Jesus Comes Again

~~~~~~

There is no point at which you can say, "Well, I'm successful now. I might as well take a nap." —Unknown.

"…And I will say to my soul, 'Soul, you have many goods laid up for many years; take your ease; eat, drink, and be merry.'" But God said to him, "Fool! This night your soul will be required of you…'so is he who lays up treasure for himself, and is not rich toward God." *—Luke 12:19-21.*

SECTION II

Serving God's Leader as Armorbearer

CHAPTER NINE

From the Heart of an Armorbearer

"Do all that you have in mind," his armorbearer said, "Go ahead; I am with you heart and soul!" —Samuel 14:7

ೞ

When God called my husband and me to serve as Armorbearers to our senior pastors, we started looking for good examples. We looked for people who have served or currently serve in the ministry of assisting. We asked the Holy Spirit, our Teacher, to give us examples. We wanted to know the qualities needed to be an effective Armorbearer.

He showed us examples in name and function. A special one comes to mind, which was not mentioned by name in the Bible, but by his function as Prince Jonathan's Armorbearer. He was not involved in the ministry of assisting anyone and everyone. He was assigned to Jonathan. He was focused and attentive to his leader.

When Jonathan is found on top of the hill spying out the enemy's camp, we don't have to look very far to find his helper. He was there with him. Scripture says Jonathan turned to his Armorbearer and said, "Let's go up ..." His assistant's response was, "Do all that is in your mind. For I am with you heart and soul." [2]

Those words are music to any leader's ears, whether he is a weary church leader or a pastor needing an arm of support. I believe the Body of

Christ needs those who will support the man or woman of God in a more tangible way. God is looking for people who will be with their assigned leader heart and soul.

A Lesson from Moses

Moses had the tremendous task of leading approximately one million Jewish slaves out of Egypt, a lot for any man. Even so, it became clear that God had his back as His design for a support team slowly unfolded. He had called Aaron and Miriam to help him.

Then he appointed the seventy elders who partook of his authority and helped him. Aaron's sons were called forward to help with the priestly duties; later the whole Levite tribe was assigned to help in the priesthood. During the battle with the Amalakites, Aaron and Hur stepped forward in unison to hold up Moses' arms in the battle, as Joshua led the troops to victory. This was the first mention of Joshua, the man who served Moses in the ministry of assisting.

In this instance, he served Moses by being a helper in the battle against God's enemies. The next event, a Holy God summoned Moses to come up the mountain; Joshua was identified as Moses' aide who went with him. He did not come down until Moses did, forty days and nights later. He was also noted for his zeal at the Tent of Meeting.

When Moses would go talk with God and return to the camp, Joshua would stay behind in the Tent. He was faithful in this ministry of helping the Lord by assisting Moses for over forty years. Moses' armorbearer Joshua inspires us with an example of a zealous assistant, giving enough intensity and focus to help his leader accomplish the impossible for God. [3]

Consider the Ministry of Assistance

Take your place as a God appointed armorbearer

There are pastors and leaders who are weary in the fight because we have not taken our place. We must take our place as God appointed Armorbearers, assistants, and helpers in His army.

God will hold us accountable for the support that should have been given if that leader fails because of it. (ITSOA pg. 64-66)

1. According to the author, building relationship you're your leader will guard you. How so, and do you agree? Write below why you agree or disagree:

_____

_____

_____

2. Each leader is different. Has the Holy Spirit taught you anything about your leader?

_____

_____

_____

3. Define loyalty. How can loyalty be displayed in an armor bearer's service to his/her leader?

_____

_____

_____

4. Describe and write below what you believe is the key to a watchful spirit.

_____

_____

5. According to the author, what are godly garments? Why is important to wear them around your leader?

_____

_____

_____

Remember These Principles

As the Holy Spirit began to teach us about armor bearing, He gave us biblical as well as modern-day illustrations. We began to see qualities to model in the most surprising places. My husband and I have an adopted member of our family that exemplifies some of the qualities needed for armor bearing.

Our dog is loyal, attentive, and his watchful nature has endeared him to us over the years. Six weeks after he was born, we received his ancestral papers and discovered he came from a long line of loyal Rottweillers. We added Domino's name to his family tree with names like Majestic Rocky Johnston, Grizzly Moon Star, Welkerhaus' Thunder, Midnight, Star, and BooBoo Bearess. Later, we took Domino to an obedience class. May I brag a little?

At that time, he was the most obedient member of the class. He sat quietly at our side with this puzzled look, observing the other dogs' behavior. There was another Rottweiller, two dogs down that wanted to bite everything in sight. The owners enrolled in the class as a final effort to bring him in control. Next to us was a huge Dalmatian that acted as if he brought his owner to class; he would not listen to anything she said. In addition, present in the class were two dogs that barked non-stop.

One of the first things our instructor told us (besides how to stop a constantly barking dog) was to bond with our dogs. We could do that by leashing the dog to our side for a day or two. Whatever we did, our dog would be at our side. His instruction was, "If someone broke in on your family you do not want your dog off chewing a shoe, not attentive that you were being attacked." In our case, somehow we had already bonded with Domino.

Whatever we did, he was right there at our side. When we put him outside to play, he would sit at the window and watch what we were doing, obviously desiring to be back inside near us.

He is the most watchful and attentive dog we have ever had. Domino offers us a pattern of the simple qualities necessary to possess as an effective Armorbearer such as loyalty, watchfulness, and attentiveness.

Another element of effective armor bearing can be the acknowledgement of God's choice. I have realized our choices have everything to do with the Lord's choice. Although the Lord knows His own and He has said, "I chose you, you did not choose yourself," we must accept the call.[4]

The moment I acknowledged myself as a God chosen Armorbearer, my self-doubts left and the anointing flowed. There are some key things to remember while growing in the ministry of armor bearing:

- **Recognize God still appoints people to help today.** Then the Lord said to Moses, "See, I have chosen Bezalel son of Uri, the son of Hur ... And I have appointed Oholiab, son of Ahisamach, of the tribe of Dan to help him."[5]

- **Allow God to make your appointment.** In observing ministry leaders and helpers alike, your assignment may not necessarily be whom you would choose. John C. Maxwell simplifies this principle saying, "Leaders attract not whom they want, but who they are."[6] Even so, God chooses and appoints, for He knows the needs of the ministry and the personalities. He fitly joins leader and helper together, if we allow Him.

- **Know your calling will be specific.** God places an Armorbearer with a designated person in leadership. Your appointment will be specific. Joshua was assigned to Moses, Elisha to Elijah, David to Saul, Timothy to Paul, etc.

- **Your leader will be worthy.** He or she will be a faithful servant with proven leadership. More than likely they will be serving in one of the fivefold offices of ministry. God will appoint you to serve one who is faithful.

- **God will give confirmation.** Let your appointment be established through two or three witnesses.[7] You and your leader will know. Don't be in a hurry. If God has truly called you to a certain person, He will give evidence of your appointment.

- **Resist pride.** It will oppose your service in the ministry of helps and God will oppose you when you are prideful. Strive to wear humility as a garment.[8]

- **Don't be surprised by persecution.** No servant is greater than his master is. Our Lord was persecuted and His godly servants will be persecuted. Rejoice that you are counted among the godly and prepare for persecution.[9]

- **Know God is your defender.** Let's purpose to choose Him as our defense as we serve others.[10] You have laid your armor down to hold another's. In the same way, Christ has said, "There is no greater love, than one to lay down his life for his friends." [11]

- **God still appoints Armorbearers to serve in the ministry of helps today.** Your leader needs you. According to Bishop T D. Jakes in his Keepers of the Flame tape series, "Many of our leaders' arms have fallen down, not because they weren't anointed, but because there was no one in place to hold their hands up in the heat of the battle."[12]

Discussion Starters

Answer the following questions for personal study and/or discuss your answers when you meet with your small group.

1. Whose support is God holding you accountable?

_____

_____

_____

2. Have you determined to develop what God has entrusted to you?

_____

_____

_____

3. Has your courage and support bolstered your leader's confidence to obey God?

_____

_____

_____

4. What qualities are needed to be an effective Armorbearer?

_____

_____

_____

5. How did God confirm your appointment as an Armorbearer to your leader?

_____

_____

Action Notes

As an administration of the helps ministry, God has uniquely formed the armor bearer's place in His support system. While teaching us about armor bearing, the Holy Spirit gave us biblical as well as modem-day illustrations.

As an exercise, find a modem-day example of an Armorbearer. Write below qualities to model from this person. Can't think of anyone? Don't forget to do what we did pray and ask God to show you examples. He will, you know.

_____

_____

_____

_____

_____

_____

_____

_____

Next Chapter

Do you believe your service as an armorbearer is a part of the ministry of Jesus? If so, you'll enjoy the next chapter *The Ministry of an Armorbearer* for it encourages you be the best helper in the Christian battle to the leader God has sent you to...

Memory Principle: Serve Believing

~~~~~~

Anything the mind can conceive and believe it can achieve. —Unknown.

Jesus said unto him, If thou canst believe, all things are possible to him that believeth. *—Mark 9:23.*

CHAPTER TEN

The Ministry of an Armorbearer

Each one should use whatever gift he has received to serve others, faithfully administering God's grace in its various forms. If anyone serves, he should do it with the strength God provides, so that in all things God may be praised through Jesus Christ. —1 Peter 4:11-12

ও

Look with me at an illustration that possibly reflects the general attitude of the Church toward a position of helps. Consider that Father God looks throughout the land (your Church) for a heart fully committed to him to use in ministry? He is developing His apostles, prophets, teachers, evangelists, and His pastors.

Now, He is looking for His ministers called to help. He has looked, prompted, and called. Nevertheless, very few seem to take Him serious. "Nah, God wouldn't be calling me to be a helper," they say, "Is it a worthy calling to only assist the leader?" I believe it is. Jesus told us that if we as His representatives only give a glass of water to a disciple of his, we would receive a disciple's reward!

A Lesson From Hur's Grandon Bezalel

In Old Testament days, God appointed Bezalel, grandson of Hur, and filled him with the Spirit of God, giving him great wisdom, ability, and skill in constructing the Tabernacle and everything in it. Alongside him, he appointed to help him Oholiab, son of Ahisamach. Moses later revealed that God had gifted Beazalel and Oholiab to teach others their skills.

Moses called a meeting and told the people to bring their offerings to God to build the Tabernacle. The Spirit of God stirred the people. Some brought materials and others supplied their time and their skills to the building of the Tabernacle. Soon, more than enough materials were gathered, and then Moses told Bezalel, Oholiab, and all others who felt called to begin work.

When it was finished, they brought the tabernacle to Moses. Moses inspected their work and blessed the Israelites for they had done just as the Lord had commanded. Each person heard the call for his or her place of service.

God then blessed them as a people for a job well done because of their unity and each individual serving where God called them. I pray that our hearts would be stirred for each to take the place God has called him to in the sanctuary, the true tabernacle set up by the Lord, not by man. [2]

Consider the Ministry of an Armorbearer

Minister as a part of the Body of Christ

Do you believe your service as an armorbearer is a part of the ministry of Jesus? If so, you'll enjoy this lesson for it encourages you be the best intercessor, assistant and helper in the battle to the leader God has sent you to.

To grow in your ministry, decide to periodically examine yourself and your actions. Am I faithful in interceding? Am I watchful in spirit? Does my Lord consider me a good ambassador of Him as well as my leader? I even examine why I am doing what I do. Maybe you do too. It is good for us to examine ourselves in this area. Each time I do this, I remember my ministry is as 'unto my Lord'.

1. When was the last time you examined your service to your leader, and what areas did you examine?

_____

_____

_____

2. Are you faithful in interceding? If not, how can you strengthen this area of ministry?

_____

_____

_____

3. Jesus said, "Watch and pray ... The spirit is willing but the flesh is weak." Do you consider yourself watchful in spirit? If not how can you increase your watchfulness?

_____

_____

_____

4. Define the term gracious.

_____

_____

_____

5. What does graciousness have to do with armor bearing?

_____

_____

_____

Remember These Principles

Do you believe your service, as an Armorbearer is a part of the ministry of Jesus? If not, change your mindset and acknowledge God has appointed you to support your leader in excellence. The writer of Revelation says, "Keep your clothes with you, that you may not be found naked and ashamed when our Lord comes."

In other words, when our Master comes, may he find us doing what He's commanded us to do? May he come quickly in the midst of our intercession for His leaders? May the Bridegroom come and find us watching. Will our Lord arrive the second time and readily say, "Well done, my good and faithful servants?" Take a closer look with me at some of the ministry functions that we as armorbearers are called to be busy doing:

God's Appointed Assistant

Then the Lord said to Moses, (See, I have chosen Bezalel son of Uri, the son of Hur ... And I have appointed Oholiab son of Ahisamach, of the tribe of Dan to assist him. "-Exodus 31:1, 6

I overheard a slightly frustrated pastor saying, "I wish my assistant could help me in protecting my designated time to study. I know she means well, but when I go into my office to study because I'm teaching that night, I need the uninterrupted time.

Even when I tell her I don't want to be interrupted, it's like I've mouthed the words with no meaning. She still allows people to enter and even ushers them in to me." She went on to say, "I wish I could give her a different mindset."

There is a different mindset to offer. There is the ministry of assisting instead of being just a good assistant, paid, or non-paid. Is there a difference? Yes. A God-appointed assistant who recognizes his or her higher calling will begin to minister to their leader with a different mindset.

- **Gain the mindset of an Armorbearer.** You are a God-appointed assistant called to support the man or woman of God. Begin to look at your assistantship as ministry unto the Lord.

- **Protect or facilitate your leaders' time.** In the book of Acts, Stephen and Phillip were among the seven assigned to take care of the details of ministry while the Apostles ministered before the Lord.

- **Discern your leader's spirit.** Sometimes your officer is operating in their God-ordained office under the anointing and other times they are just being themselves. Respect them in either. When it's time to relax with your leader, be a good friend and relax. When it's time to take care of the Father's business and His people, slip back into the working mode with them.

- **Guard against familiarity.** Familiarity will affect how others look at your leader. If you are being too familiar at inappropriate times, it will cause respect for your leader to drain. Remain respectful of authority.

- **Be a gracious representative.** Know that in your serving, you are representing God and your officer. If you have to defer someone to protect your leaders' time, (as in the example given above), be gracious. You can be gentle but firm with God's sheep.

- **Be one of their strongest allies.** Show that you are always for them. In word and action, support your authority. If you discover criticism in others, work to show the good side or intention of your leader's heart.

If you haven't considered your assistantship as ministry in a while, or perhaps ever, surprise your leader, begin to handle things differently, take on the attitude of a minister of helps. Let your assisting become the ministry of assisting.

Intercessions of an Armorbearer

And I sought for a man among them that should make up the hedge, and stand in the gap before me for the land –EzekieI22:30a

A description of an intercessor is one called to take the place of another, to stand in the gap, or as one of our pastors said, "Stand in the way." She says an evil spirit said to her as she interceded for our Senior Pastor's wife, "She's in the way, and I can't get to her husband because she's always praying for him."

Yes, God called us to be in the way of the enemy's plan for our leader's demise. As we pray, we are often able to stop the plans of the enemy or at least scatter his efforts. God somehow multiplies the odds when we pray for our leaders. Remember, one will put a thousand to flight and two will make ten thousand flee.

In operating as an Armorbearer one must develop the characteristics of an intercessor. As a part of the divine call to minister in helps, comes a divine call to intercede for our leaders.[3] Allow the Holy Spirit to develop in you the heart of intercession. As an intercessor, one must possess:

- **Willingness.** The intercessor must be willing to pray when the Holy Spirit asks.

- **Obedience.** God's intercessors will be faithful to follow through on the promptings to pray for our leaders.

- **Confidentiality.** Can God trust you with the inner chambers of His house (the Church)? He may show you confidential things to pray about your leader. One operating in the true spirit of armor bearing can be trusted to pray for his leader in confidential matters.

- **Perseverance.** Do you pray until you get a release to stop? Do not give up on God's leader; He is not through with her or him either. Pray until the victory comes! The Holy Spirit is faithful to let you know.

Are you involved in intercession for your leader? Good! Don't let our Father God have to look beyond you to find a faithful intercessor for your leader. Be the man or woman faithful to pray.

Helpers in the Battle

These are they that came to David to Ziklag, while he yet concealed himself because of Saul the son of Kish; they were among the mighty men, his helpers in War. -1 Chronicles 12:1 standing in the gap and making up the hedge for God's leader.

I believe many of the same principles apply to spiritual warfare as natural warfare. I have been asked by one of my milder friends of faith, "Why are you so militant in your faith, Earma? I prefer a quiet church service with quiet prayers, not so much celebration, and noise."

Without hesitation I responded, "I respect your beliefs, but I have learned if you are a human being you are in the war of good and evil. I know there is a God and He is a good God. On the other hand, I know there is a devil and he's a bad devil. Especially if you are a Christian, the devil treats you as if you are a threat to his kingdom. If you are a praying Christian, whether you know it or not, you are a threat to the devil's kingdom.

I realize while we sing, whether it is quiet or loud, our enemy, the devil, has launched military strategies against the success of our life. In the same breath, I must assert that Jesus has already paid the price for the world by His death on the cross. And with all my strength, I enforce that victory in my life and others through prayer."

David's mighty men offer a good example of Armorbearers being helpers in the war. The descriptions given in Scripture of David's mighty men will give us insight to the qualities God is building in His mighty men and women in New Testament days. Go with me to First Chronicles 12:1-40 and review some of the descriptions given to describe the helpers.[4] Verse 8 describes the Gadites who came over to help as:

- **Valiant (brave warriors).** The writer of Hebrews describes our strength as small in the day of battle if we faint. It has helped me tremendously in my faith to remember the words of Joyce Meyers, one of the mothers of practical faith, "If you are afraid, do it afraid. Just obey God."

- **Ready (trained for war).** Are you allowing Father God to discipline (train) or ready you? When Moses started out with the Israelites, they were not that far from the Promised Land.

  However, knowing the newly released slaves were not ready for battle, God took them through a longer route through the wilderness. He wanted to purge them, care for them, and simply prepare them for the victories that lay ahead.

  As Biblical history tells us, the Israelites complained, disobeyed, and resisted their God into a judgment that lasted 40 years. Which brings us back to my original question rephrased, "Are you allowing Father God to lead you through the longer routes in life to ready you for your victories?"

- **Able (skillful in handling shield and spear).** Scripture tells us that the Gadite men were skilled, experienced, and even talented with handling their weapons of war. As a new Christian, I often dreamed of myself fighting our enemy the devil with brooms, sticks, dull knives or anything ineffective.

  Finally, I got tired of being beat up in life and my dreams, which I'm sure you've recognized was only a symbolic mirror of what was happening in my life.

  My Lord began to train me with our weapons that are not carnal (fleshly and ineffective), but mighty to the pulling down of the enemy's strongholds. He constantly walked me through Ephesians [6] until when I would receive a flashback of my battles I would see myself welding the shield of faith and skillfully using the sword (the Word of God), cutting the enemy's head off and ripping him to pieces.

  The writer of Ephesians encourages us to be strong (able, skillful, effective) in the Lord and in His mighty power. As we stand against the schemes of the devil for our lives and our leader's life, he further instructs us to put on the full armor of God.

- **Leaders (the least was match for a hundred and the greatest for a thousand).** I believe the captain warriors of Gadite had entered into God's multiplication of power. No wonder the enemy fights our unity in marriages, families, holy partnerships and ultimately the Body of Christ. He knows what happens to his kingdom every time faith is exercised in the God that multiplies the odds against him.

  Look at some of the Biblical examples of this divine phenomenon: Gideon and his greatly reduced army (300) defeated an uncounted number of men.5 Jonathan and his Armorbearer defeated several war parties and an army of men.

  Jesus fed approximately 10,000 people with two loaves and five fish. Prophet Isaiah said, "One would cause a thousand to flee and two would put 10,000 to flight." Take the lead in God's great army knowing that the God we serve multiplies our odds against the enemy.

- **Fierce (face of a lion).** Have you seen Reggie White's game-face (attitude), as he looks at the opposing team? There is no doubt in the opposing team's mind that they are about to get steam-rolled, if possible.

  In a similar way, we are to wear the face (attitude) of the lion towards our enemy. A number of the defining terms of fierce are bold, intense, and violent. These words confirm what our attitude should be in faith toward the devil's intrusion in our lives and our leader's life.

- **Swift (gazelle on the mountain).** Earlier in this book, we spoke briefly of maintaining a sense of urgency in developing the spirit of armor bearing. I believe our God wants this quality developed in His servants more. He wants us to remember the time is short.

  Jesus imparting the sense of urgency to His disciples said, "All of us must quickly (swiftly) carry out the tasks assigned us by the one who sent Me, for there is little time left before the night falls and all work comes to an end." [6] In light of this, let us be like gazelles upon the mountain in carrying out our assignments before God.

Discussion Starters

Answer the following questions for your personal study and/or discuss your answers when you meet with your small group study.

1. Do you consider your position of armorbearing a commission?

_____

_____

_____

2. Have you committed to pray the prayer of intercession for your leader?

_____

_____

_____

3. Has God stirred you to action lately?

_____

_____

_____

4. How did the lesson about Bezalel and Oholiab demonstrate the call to assistantship ministry?

_____

_____

_____

5. Explain how your assistantship is considered ministry?

_____

_____

_____

Action Notes

Your leader or pastor is a busy person. If they were not they would not need your help as an assistant, right? With so many things to do and take care of, our priorities will sometimes become misaligned. We seek to balance our lives and our leader's lives while keeping a gracious attitude.

I have discovered when I keep my priorities in line, balance is more easily achieved. You know the priorities I am speaking of: God first, spouse, children, work and church, etc.

As an exercise of balance, list your top task (priorities) and answer the following questions. What is required of me? What task can I delegate to someone else? What tasks can be stopped altogether? Who will hold me accountable to my top priorities? Discuss the results of this exercise and any need for balance or re-alignment of priorities with your class.

1. Top Tasks:

_____

_____

_____

_____

_____

_____

_____

_____

2. What is required of me?

_____

_____

3. What task can I delegate to someone else?

_____

_____

4. What task can be stopped altogether?

_____

_____

5. Who will hold me accountable of my top priority tasks.

_____

_____

6. Do I see the need for balance in my priorities?

_____

_____

Next Chapter

Have you noticed that much of how we respond to life's ups and downs has to do with our character? God desires to build character in us. In the next chapter *Developing the Character of Christ* we discuss character that will help carry the anointing God has entrusted us with.

Memory Principle: Serve Just Doing It!

~~~~~~

Waste no more time thinking about the good you should do. Just do it. *—Unknown.*

I'll show you my faith by what I do. *—James 2: 18b.*

CHAPTER ELEVEN

Developing the Character of Christ

And even though Jesus was God's Son, He had to learn from experience what it was like to obey; when obeying meant problems and difficulties. —Hebrews 5:8 TLB

ଔ

Have you noticed that much of how we respond to life's circumstances has to do with our character? God desires to build character within us. He desires to train (discipline) us as His children.1 Training and disciplining does not always feel good. In fact, it can be downright painful.

A Lesson from Prophet Samuel

Little Samuel was helping the Lord by assisting Eli. In fact, his mother, Hannah, had consecrated him for service in the house of God since before birth. The man of God, Eli, and his sons showed a lack of character. The times were dark for God's people and character seemed to be lacking in most.

Yet the scripture tells us Samuel grew in favor with God and with man to the point that God let none of his words fall to the ground void. The apostle James told us, "The man who claims to be religious and yet, does not bridle his tongue is not as he claims to be."

We can pattern our service after the young Samuel who grew in favor with God and man by developing character. He left us a certain example of being the Lord's helper by serving Eli. His words matched his actions so much that God could always perform His will and word through Samuel.6

Consider the Character of Christ

Build character one good choice at a time.

Have you noticed that much of how we respond to life's ups and downs has to do with our character? God desires to build character in us. Character that will help carry the anointing he has entrusted us with. Study with us as we build character choice by choice.

We desire people of character in our churches, our cities, our countries, and our world. Most if not all of the success stories turned failures in recent years, have been partially due to lack of character. No one can rise above the limitations of his character.

1. Name a right choice you have made which resulted in character?

_____

_____

_____

2. How does your character preach the gospel?

_____

_____

_____

3. The Bible says, "Bad company corrupts good character." What does good character do? Write the Scripture *Hebrews 5:8 TLB* out below:

_____

_____

_____

5. How does this verse above apply to us as Christians?

_____

_____

_____

Remember These Principles

Allow Father God to develop character in you through the ministry of assisting. Character is vital to our ability to carry the anointing God has for His army. The world's nations can fall and rise based on the character of its leaders. Just as much and more, our leaders in the Kingdom of God are operating with the character built in their season of serving. When you choose humility instead of what others think, you should know that in your ministry of service you are building moral strength.

Each time you walk: in love instead of retaliation or revenge, I assure you your character has grown. Choosing patience with the will of God instead of doing it your own way will build the strong faith you desire. Cooperate with God as He endeavors to build character in you through your armor bearing.

People without inner strength cannot be counted on day after day because their ability to perform changes constantly. If people do not know what to expect from you, at some point they lose faith in you. Character inspires several things in the people around us. Character inspires:

- **Consistency.** Billy Graham is a man that communicates consistency in our modem world. In his life, he has consistently shown humility, compassion, and godly integrity. From the White House to the street, people have observed his consistent godly living and compassion for lost souls. Your consistency will inspire hope and faith in a world that sees so little.

- **Trust.** Psychologists agree that we earn trust. Which is why most people do not give their trust to just anyone. A pastor friend of mine said, "I trust people until they give me a reason not to." I responded with, "That's wonderful, but I don't trust until a person gives me a reason to trust them." Whatever your struggle, your character will inspire trust in those around you.

- **Favor.** Remember Prophet Samuel grew in favor with man and God because of his character. In addition, Jesus, our chief example, grew in favor with God and with man. My former jail ministry leader used to admonish us to follow the rules of the authorities of each prison facility because of the favor involved.

  Our adherence to the rules built an atmosphere where the officials and attendants favored us and wanted to cooperate. The integrity and character of the ministry team built trust and respect. Grow in favor with God and man because you submit to the authorities in your life.

Join me as we determine to be like David's mighty men in believing and discerning the times (last days) in which we live. We need character in our ministers and in our leaders of the faith. We need character developed in our servants of the house.

If God has appointed you to walk as an armorbearer to one of our leaders, know that character can be developed through this position. David's mighty men again offer us exemplary qualities that will support God's anointing.

The writer of Chronicles describes the gathering of God's Old Testament army, "For at that time day by day men kept coming to David to help him, until there was a great army, like the army of God, [7] In the same way, I see men and women all over the Body of Christ saying, Aha! This is my time.

This is my appointed place until the Body of Christ will be the great army of God in which He has called us to be in these last days. The same character that was noted in David's mighty men will be developed in us as we each take our place in God's army today. Listed below are other commendable qualities mentioned by the writer of Chronicles in verses 32 and 38:

- **Understanding (understood the times).** These men understood the season and the time in which they lived. Jesus rebuked the Pharisees' unbelief in His day saying, "You see and understand the changes of the weather by the clouds or the sun shining brightly with no clouds. Yet you refuse to look and understand the times you are living in."

- **Wisdom (knew what to do).** The mighty men of David were wise and knew what to do. Let us be wise and discerning in knowing what to do in the Body of Christ. Find your place and do what God has called you to do. Be the men and women of purpose that the Father God has said we are.

- **Loyalty (single-minded, fully determined).** Are you fully determined in your place of service? Only then can we be single-minded and loyal to our leaders. The Apostle Paul gave us wisdom about maintaining the mindset of a soldier when fulfilling loyalty during difficult seasons, "Endure hardship with us like a good soldier of Christ Jesus." [8] Decide with me to be loyal and serve single-mindedly as God's great armorbearers.

- **Volunteerism (could keep rank, good follower).** Good soldiers have no problem with keeping rank. They know their designated spot and follow in place. If we as God's army of volunteers would apply the same principle, we would not break rank but follow our leaders as they follow Christ.

- **Unity (of one mind and purpose).** God knew the power of unity and working in one purpose when He confused the people building the tower of Babel Just as Satan knows the power we would exercise as one in Christ, he strives to create confusion and division in our midst. Pray with me for the unity of the Body of Christ, as our Lord prayed for the unity of His followers that we might accomplish His will.

Once more, I must say it seems our Father God is painstakingly involved in working character in us. However, it is up to us to work with him so that we may reap the harvest of righteousness he longs to give us.

Discussion Starters

Answer the following questions for personal study and/or discuss your answers when you meet with your armorbearer's class.

1. Have you realized you are the Lord's helper if you are assisting your appointed leader? How so?

_____

_____

_____

2. Has God desired to know what you would do through a difficult choice?

_____

_____

_____

3. What character quality do you believe God is working in you now and are you cooperating?

_____

_____

_____

4. Define the term consistency?

_____

_____

_____

5. The author states consistency will inspire hope & faith. How does consistency affect you as an armorbearer?

_____

_____

_____

Action Notes

Looking back, one of my choices in a former corporate workplace demonstrated my character. Of course like most people when faced with a choice, character was not on my mind.

Simply put, I withdrew my money contributed to purchase our manager's birthday gift. I discovered my department leaders changed their mind about the roses they planned to get her. They now planned to hire a theme stripper for her and the department's viewing pleasure...I was ridiculed and persecuted for my choice. As an exercise, describe below a choice you made in which you demonstrated character.

_____

_____

_____

_____

_____

_____

Next Chapter:

We'll study in the next chapter: *Be an Anticipator of Needs.* To anticipate the needs of your leader, you must first be attentive and a good listener with the Holy Spirit. Continue to the next chapter and make a point to be willing, prayerful, ready and quiet to anticipate.

Memory Principle: Serve Prepared

~~~~~~

The secret of success in life is for a man to be ready for his time when it comes. —Benjamin Disraeli.

If a man cleanses himself from the dishonorable, he will be an instrument for honorable purposes, made holy, useful to the Master and prepared to do any good work. —*2 Timothy 2:21.*

CHAPTER TWELVE

Becoming an Anticipator

And it shall come to pass before they call I will answer; while they are still speaking I will hear. —Isaiah 65:24

℗

Earlier, in chapter nine, I mentioned that I asked the Holy Spirit to show me how to be an effective Armorbearer, the kind that walks worthy of his or her calling. At the time I received this teaching, I was talking to the Lord more about my needs and desires.

I asked Him about a particular need of mine and He responded by pointing to my leader's needs. He began to show me how to anticipate those of my leader. Why is this important? I believe because He promised, "Before they call I will answer..."¹ We can be excited and honored that God would use us as a tool to fulfill His promise!

A Lesson from Mary

It was an important dinner held in the honor of Jesus at the home of special friends. Jesus would come out of the city Jerusalem to visit this home, leaving the plots and plans of His enemies behind for a few hours, knowing that His day of trials was almost upon Him.

He lounged at the table with Lazarus, the man he had raised from the dead. Martha was busy serving. Mary (Martha and Lazarus' sister) took nard (perfume) worth a year of wages and anointed Jesus. The fragrance filled the whole house. As it is with all true service and worship, it moves people.

One may be moved with compassion or another with criticism when observing a true servant. In the case of Jesus', team treasurer, he left no doubt in anyone's mind which emotion he yielded to after sharply criticizing them for allowing such a waste of funds that could have gone to the poor.

Jesus, knowing the motives of Judas's heart, rebuked him saying, "Leave her alone she is the only one that has anticipated my need for anointing before burial (He had told his followers on several occasions of His death in a few days).

As a memorial of this act, she will always be mentioned in the gospel." Mary offers us a beautiful example of service that has anticipated her leader's need. With the help of the Holy Spirit, we can worship our God by anticipating the need of our appointed leader.[3]

Consider the Anticipation of Needs

Learn to anticipate your leader's needs.

To anticipate the needs of your leader, you must first be attentive and a good listener with the Holy Spirit. Read this lesson and continue to be willing, prayerful, ready and quiet to anticipate.

In God's kingdom, to increase something, you usually decrease. Jesus instructed us in this matter with, "Whoever finds his life will lose it, and whoever loses his life for My sake will find it."

1. Define anticipation:

_____

_____

_____

2. To be an anticipator the author states one must be attentive and a good listener with the Holy Spirit. Is there anything else you would like to add about being an anticipator?

_____

_____

_____

3. Describe one important lesson the Holy Spirit has taught you about armor bearing?

_____

_____

_____

4. Define prudence:

_____

_____

_____

5. Give an example in which prudence was required?

_____

_____

_____

Remember These Principles

To anticipate the needs of your leader, you must first be attentive and a good listener with the Holy Spirit. To be attentive to the Holy Spirit, you are called to be willing, prayerful, ready and quiet in spirit.

- **Willing.** Are you willing to anticipate another's need? A part of anticipation includes laying your needs aside to attend to another. You may be praying for your leaders while your needs seemingly go unmet. Not so. God takes care of the faithful.

- **Prayerful.** Prayer prepares your spirit to hear God. Remain prayerful and walk in the Spirit.

- **Ready.** Stay ready for the Holy Spirit to prompt you. If you get distracted or have to stop to do something else, you will miss the time of anticipation.

- **Quiet.** Remaining quiet in spirit is not always easy for talkative or quiet personalities. Your task may be taming your tongue in your mouth or putting a harness on the thoughts in your mind. Either way, if you are always talking you may miss the Holy Spirit's directions. Sssh!

Discussion Starters

Answer the following questions for personal study and/or discuss your answers when you meet with your armor bearer's class.

1. Are your actions of service fragrant with worship of your God?

_____

_____

_____

2. Do you consider yourself an instrument of the Lord?

_____

_____

_____

3. What must you put down, take off, or put away to walk: the narrow path of servant hood?

_____

_____

_____

4. Explain to a new armorbearer what quiet-in-spirit means?

_____

_____

_____

5. How do you develop quietness in spirit?

_____

_____

_____

Action Notes

After defining anticipation and what the author believes is a call to other Armorbearers to begin to walk in anticipation with their leaders. Has God used you to anticipate your leader's needs? If so, describe the experience below. If not, as a part of the exercise pray and ask God to reveal to you how. Write the results below:

_____

_____

_____

_____

_____

_____

_____

_____

_____

Next Chapter:

All Scripture is useful for instruction and example. Read the next chapter: *The Gehazi Factor* to point the way through biblical scripture to what to do and what to not do as an armorbearer.

Memory Principle: Serve to Provoke (Spur) Others to Good

~~~~~~

Treat people as if they were what they ought to be, and you help them to become what they are capable of being. —Johan Wolfgang Von Goethe.

And let us consider how we may spur one another on toward love and good works. —*Hebrews 10:24.*

CHAPTER THIRTEEN

THE GEHAZI FACTOR

Gehazi, the servant of Elisha the man of God, said to himself, "My master was too easy on Naaman, this Aramean, by not accepting from him what he brought. As surely as the Lord lives, I will run after him and get something from him." —*2 Kings 5:20 NIV*

☙

I have discovered all Scripture is useful for instruction and example. Our Bible does not hold back in showing us examples of what not to do! In this chapter we look at some examples of wrong choices and disobedience in Scripture.

A Lesson Gehazi

The young man, Gehazi started out as an obedient assistant to Elisha the prophet. However, later he succumbed to the temptation of covetousness and familiarity. When Naaman, a foreigner, who God healed through Elisha's ministry, offered gifts, the man of God refused the reward lest it be thought a foreigner could come and buy a miracle from the God of Israel.

Gehazi thinking to himself that his master had been too easy on the foreigner ran after him to see what he could get. He lied to Naaman, received $4,000 and two suits of clothing, returned home and hid the gifts. When he returned to work, Elisha confronted him. Because of Gehazi's attitude and disobedience, the leprosy that Naaman was healed of came on him and his descendants.

Gehazi's familiarity and covetousness resulted in the loss of his respect and reverence for the office of prophet. This story offers an example of what not to do in serving your leader.[2]

Consider Obedience

Develop a spirit of obedience to God

All Scripture is useful for instruction and example. This lesson will point the way through Biblical Scripture to what to do and what to not do as an armorbearer. Jesus said to His disciples, "If you love me you will obey me."

1. Write the scripture 1 Peter 5:6 below:

_____

_____

_____

2. Who is responsible for the humbling mentioned in the scripture above?

_____

_____

_____

3. Define criticism and blessing:

_____

_____

4. Which of the qualities above do you see more of in your life?

_____

_____

_____

5. Define complacency and zeal:

_____

_____

_____

Remember These Principles

When God has called you to be an Armorbearer or anything else, your faith will be tested. The question will be asked, "Are you really called by God?" Circumstances will pose the question, "Will you continue?" Satan and his imps have designed circumstances to take us off course. Here are a few things to guard against as we endeavor to stay on God's course of servant hood:

- **Guard against the spirit of familiarity.** You can become so familiar in relationship that you lose your reverence and respect for the office in which your leader serves. David never lost the reverence for the ordained office of kingship. Even when his king no longer deserved respect, he continued to respect God's man and his office.

- **Don't confuse what belongs to your leader as belonging to you.** Many times as servants of the Lord, we begin to realize we are chosen vessels of His. With this realization may come the opportunity to become confused about what belongs to us? The enemy's bait becomes, "YOU have worked so closely with your leader, you can do better than him or her. God called you, too. He speaks to you ...

"I encourage you to remember where God placed you. Remain there until God moves you. Miriam, sister to Moses, fell for this dangerous thought pattern. She began to complain with her brother Aaron, "Doesn't God speak to us, also?" She received leprosy because of her sins of insubordination and criticism. Her brother, Moses, prayed and she received her healing.

- **Determine to be yourself.** It is wise to be obedient and agreeable. It is not wise to lose your personality and become false. Remain unpretentious in your relationships. Allow your leader to be himself or herself, but never pretend.

- **Acknowledge relationship boundaries.** There are normal boundaries that are set by what kind of relationship you enjoy with your leader. For example, if you had a predecessor in serving your appointed leader, allow time to get to know each other. Do not try to be that person to them.

- **Avoid competition.** Do not compete with your leader's family, ministry associates or other close associates. When I learned that we each have a place in God's kingdom and in the ministry, I ceased to strive for a position. I began to know and fulfill my place and my function as a minister.

Discussion Starters

Answer the following questions during your personal study and discuss your answers when you meet with your small group study.

1. Have you been baited for offense lately? If so, briefly describe the experience and your response.

_____

_____

_____

2. Have you committed the sin of criticism of your authority? If so, briefly describe.

_____

_____

_____

3. Have you ever confused what belonged to your leader as yours?

_____

_____

_____

4. How has your faith been tested in armor bearing?

_____

_____

_____

5. Define the term continue and describe any opportunities to give up on armor bearing?

_____

_____

Action Notes

Read the story of Gehazi, Naaman & Elisha again in 2 Kings 5:20-27. List the negative qualities and actions of Gehazi that got him into trouble.

_____

_____

_____

_____

_____

Next Chapter:

Do you consider yourself courageous? It takes courage to be faithful. It takes strength to swim up stream when most everyone around you is swimming downstream. Study the next chapter: *Daring to Be Faithful* to show yourself approved and gain courage for when you need it.

Other Resources:

Don't forget to consider becoming a part of our web community http://www.armorbearers.net for further encouragement and insightful information. Visit our new Bible study forum at http://www.armorbearers.net/forums/ to post your comments or sign-up for one of the FREE courses and interact with others from around the world.

Memory Principle: Serve with Order In All Things

~~~~~~

Good order is the foundation of all things. –Edmund Burke

God is a God not of disorder, but of peace. -1 Corinthians 14:33

CHAPTER FOURTEEN

Daring to Be Faithful

God is not unrighteous to forget your work and labour of love which you have shown toward His name. –Hebrews 6:10

☙

Faithfulness can be considered as longevity. Faithfulness is staying for the long haul. Fulfilling our commitment accomplishes faithfulness. It takes courage to be faithful. It takes stamina to swim upstream when many are drifting downstream.

God honors faithfulness in any service to Him. Buddy Bell, in his Ministry of Helps handbook says, "God called my faithfulness my crowbar, and then commanded me to use it." [2] Our God is one who remembers the righteous and faithful to a thousand generations.

A Lesson from Abraham

Abraham was called God's friend, yet he was as completely human with similar passions as you or me. For example, out of fear he lied to a king about his wife, Sarah, being his sister. He almost destroyed a whole kingdom, when the King took Sarah for his own.

In mercy, God showed the king what he had done wrong then he promptly let her go. Even with Abraham's human makeup and tendencies, God declared him faithful. Abraham showed he believed God by his obedience beyond his mistakes, shortcomings, and difficult choices.

He was called faithful by what he continued to do as well as what he believed. God finally said of him, "I know him (Abraham); he is faithful. He will teach his children and all those with him how to be faithful. I can trust him to keep My ways and I will do all that I promised him." Abraham's example inspires us to be faithful in what we do in spite of our mistakes and shortcomings.[3]

Consider Faithfulness

"You are the called and the chosen now be faithful."

Do you consider yourself courageous? It takes courage to be faithful. It takes strength to swim up stream when most everyone around you is swimming downstream. Study this lesson to show yourself approved and gain courage for when you need it.

God's faithfulness is our shield and rampart. Yet, He has commanded His ministers (those entrusted with the secret things of God) to be faithful. Jeremiah put it this way, "God is looking throughout the land to find someone with their heart fully committed to Him to show Himself strong on their behalf."

1. Define faithfulness and loyalty.

_____

_____

_____

2. How does laziness and selfishness work against faithfulness?

_____

_____

_____

3. How does loyalty and perseverance nurture faithfulness?

_____

_____

_____

4. Define Perseverance:

_____

_____

_____

5. The author names at least 5 enemies to faithfulness as offenses, pride, laziness, selfishness and impatience. Which have you battled against the most in your life and service?

_____

_____

_____

Remember These Principles

God has promised blessings for the faithful. We can choose to be faithful. It is, one of the few things, we can offer our Lord. He has given us the gift of salvation, the gift of His Holy Spirit. It is His good pleasure to give us His kingdom. We can be faithful to Jesus and His ministry.

Additionally, God remembers the faithful. Hebrew 6:10 encourages us with, "God is not unrighteous to forget your work and labor of love (faithfulness), which you have shown toward His name." [4] Here are a few promises in Scripture to remember about faithfulness:

- *To the faithful you show yourself faithful, to the blameless you show yourself blameless, to the pure you show yourself pure. Psa.18:25*

- *Love the Lord, all His saints! The Lord preserves the faithful. Psa.31:23a*

- *For He guards the lives of His faithful ones. –Psa. 97:10b*

- *You have been faithful with a few things; I will put you in charge of many things. –Mt. 25:23b*

More Principles

- **Satan is an enemy to our faithfulness.** He hates it when we are faithful. I think because it reflects a faithful God to a faithless world. Therefore, it is no surprise when he sets traps and distractions to draw us from our God-ordained path. In our case, he wants to divert us from our path of service. Beware of these baits and traps of Satan.

- **Offenses are the bait of Satan to get one off the path of faithfulness in God.** Faithfulness resists offenses. Satan will seek to trap you in unforgiveness toward a person. However, remember we always have a choice; we can be offended or forgive. Forgiveness is the right choice.

  Be alert to this trap because most people that have been trapped do not even realize it. Stay in tune with the Holy Spirit, for He will point out any baits of Satan making sure you are aware to make the right choice.

- **Pride can be very subtle in its diversion.** I found myself listening to a woman confessing her discovery of pride in her life. She admitted to saying to her leader, "I have a degree in engineering and I am not going to continue in my volunteering in the Church if all you have for me to do is collating and copying."

She later repented and continued faithfully helping wherever she was needed. When we are attentive to the Holy Spirit and careful to judge ourselves concerning pride, we will never be on the outside of the call and destiny God has planned for us.

• **Laziness and selfishness are twin enemies to the development of God's faithfulness in our life.** Allowing negative emotions and feelings to dictate our behavior rather than commitment will result in laziness. "I don't feel like it tonight. My leader will just have to make it without me..."is a common and selfish train of thought. When our fleshly desires threaten to rise up and take control, we are to offer a living sacrifice of our bodies.[5] Then we will rise to the level of commitment we are called to as faithful servants of the most high God.

• **Impatience is a sure enemy to faithfulness.** My friends who I mentioned in an earlier chapter grew weary of waiting for their appointed leader to acknowledge their gifts and talents. They felt they should have been recommended for leadership. They did not want to hear my advice of, "I'm sure it will happen in God's timing. You are excellent candidates for leadership."

They replied, "Posh! God already knows about us and we are giving our leader six months to recognize us; if not, we are out of here." Their leader did not, and they left. Later, they came back, admitted they were wrong, and should have waited. The writer of Hebrews encourages us with, "You have need of patience, and so after you have done the will of God you may receive his promise." [6]

Discussion Starters

Answer the following questions for personal study and/or discuss your answers when you meet with your small group.

1. Have you counted the cost of your ministry?

_____

_____

_____

2. Does your faith statement include continue?

_____

_____

_____

3. Has your loyalty passed any test?

_____

_____

_____

4. Name at least 5 other enemies to faithfulness:

_____

_____

_____

5. Explain how impatience works against faithfulness?

_____

_____

_____

Action Notes

Find someone considered faithful in your community and/or church? Let them know you and others consider them faithful. Then interview them asking the following questions. Write the answers below:

_____

_____

_____

_____

_____

_____

1. What has most contributed to your ability to remain faithful?

_____

_____

_____

2. What do you consider the enemies to faithfulness are?

_____

_____

_____

3. What's your best advice to someone wanting to be faithful?

_____

_____

4. Name one important test when you resisted giving up?

_____

_____

_____

5. Name one important time you chose to be faithful in spite of your mistake or shortcomings?

_____

_____

_____

Next Chapter:

Do you feel led to implement the ministry of armorbearing in your church? But like many other pastors and leaders you are searching for some guidance on just how to do that. If so, read the advice and suggestions in the following section: *The Ministry of Practical Service.*

Memory Principle: Serve with a Spirit of Completion

~~~~~~

Be like a postage stamp. Stick to one thing until you get there. —Josh Billings.

I have fought the good fight, I have finished the race, and I have kept the faith. —*2 Timothy 4:7.*

SECTION III

The Ministry of Practical Service

CHAPTER FIFTEEN

8 Highly Practical Things to Do for Your Pastor

Excellence is a habit. —Unknown

૭૪

Did you know the Los Angeles Times reported a year or so ago that "People are leaving the ministry in droves because it's too difficult." Whether we agree with that assessment or not, we can know our leaders are targeted like never before.

Remember the spiritual principle that our enemy the devil has used against God's leaders' century after century, "If you strike a shepherd, the sheep will scatter." So it stands to reason that our leaders are the number one public enemy on Satan's hit list.

On that note, it's time for a revival of honor for our leaders. It's time for the Body of Christ to rally in support of our church leaders like never before. Whether you serve as a personal Armorbearer or a volunteer in the ministry as a helper in another capacity, every leader needs support.

Even more, they want practical help from their supporters. Your service matters. To put the stamp of excellence on your service as an Armorbearer, take these eight highly practical tips in serving and tailor them for your ministry.

1. Prepare Yourself. Pray before you serve. Ask God's blessing on your service or work. Treat your service as ministry and you will find that others will more readily respect what you do. Groom yourself properly. If not uniformed, dress in the nicest Sunday Wear attire you have. Represent Christ and your leader well.

2. Arrive Before Your Pastor and Prepare His/Her Pre-Service Area. Show your prudence and respect for their ministerial duties by preparing early (before they arrive.) In other words, you don't want to be in the middle of preparation when they get there. Your goal is to greet them with an (I-am-prepared-to-serve-you) or practically speaking, do whatever you need me to do attitude.

3. Set atmosphere of pre-service area or green room. Light candles. Spray air freshener in the room. Straighten or clean room/area, if needed. Play Christian instrumental or soft praise/worship music in room, if appropriate. Some leaders may want quietness and solitude before ministering and others may feel encouraged by worship music (softly playing in background.)

4. Prepare light refreshments for leader, family and/or guests in pre-service area or green room. Setup simple buffet of refreshments as your church can afford. *Suggestions:* Bottled water, Coffee, Tea, Other Hot/Cold Beverages, Breath Mints, and Gum. Always have bottled water on hand. *Additional suggestions:* If you have several services, consider providing light breakfast if leader prefers, instant oatmeal, simple in-season fruit tray, cold cereals, juices, etc.

5. Welcome leader and family. Greet leader wearing the garments of Christ. Practically speaking, always wear a good attitude. It's amazing how easily our attitudes are transferred. Not saying your leader is weak-minded or easily influenced. But if you come in a bad mood with a critical spirit it may transfer to them. Don't have it where your leader has to guard against picking up bad attitudes from you. Wear gentleness, kindness, prayerfulness, quietness, good reports, encouraging words and so on.

6. Escort your leader and/or family to pre-service area or respective areas. I know that sounds rather formal. But we simply mean for you to walk them in, be available as opposed to greeting them and then going your separate way. Take their books, bag (if they allow or prefer) and place in a safe place.

Many ministers get particular about releasing their Bible to someone that doesn't respectfully place it in a safe place. (Not easily knocked over, easily accessible, in their view, etc.) Offer to take their children, if they have any, to their designated place - nursery, children's church, sanctuary.

Afterwards designate a place for you to stand quietly on post. Be available but not too talkative or distracting. Meaning it's not a time for you to sit and socialize with your pastor. Stay in a ministry mode.

7. Wear the mark of a true armorbearer. The mark of a true armorbearer is the spirit of Christ. The spirit of Christ working through us is humble, not self-seeking but working to the good of all. With the Spirit of Christ one would not bring unnecessary attention to oneself.

The Spirit of Christ is not conspicuous, not counting oneself equal but taking on the nature of a servant. The Spirit of Christ will work to keep and maintain the peace. It is not competitive spirited. Nor will the Spirit of Christ show itself as prideful, showy or puffed up. Simply put be humble.

8. Stay until your leader leaves. Remain available until your leader has left the building. Pick up children from designated areas. Escort pastor and/or family from building. **Additional Suggestion:** If appropriate, prepare light refreshments for after service.

If your pastor has ministered in several services, they may welcome a refreshing beverage and some light bite-size foods. Not junk food. Cut vegetables, left-over fruit from morning, crackers or whatever their preference might be. Set a good example for others, clean up afterwards. Make sure your work area is free of trash, food, serving trays, and other things.

On a final note, we encourage you to be consistent. Don't be an ON one day and OFF the next day kind of servant. For example, you start out excited and passionate about serving your pastor. You implement greeting him or her as a part of your strategy of serving in excellence. You greet them enthusiastically a couple of Sundays and then they don't see you for the next 2 or 3 times.

Don't let that be your example. Consistency is crucial; for you will begin your legacy of faithfulness by simply consistently taking care of the details. Surprise your leader! Put these highly practical tips and suggestions into practice and watch your service as an Armorbearer go to new levels with a stamp of excellence.

Disclaimer: Please know these tips in this article are just suggestions. They may be implemented as the leadership or authorities in your church allow. Be creative but complement any rules of the House and stay within authority guidelines of church organization. Remember, the mark of a true Armorbearer is the Spirit of Christ. No official title or duty list is really needed to serve like Christ did.

Memory Principle: Serve Running the Race with an Understanding of Endurance

~~~~~~

Perseverance is not a long race; it is many short races one after another.
—Walter Elliott

Run with endurance the race that's set before you. *—Hebrews 12:1.*

CHAPTER SIXTEEN

8 Highly Practical Prayers to Pray for Your Pastor

Therefore I exhort first of all that supplications, prayers, intercessions, and giving of thanks be made for all men, for kings and all who are in authority, that we may lead a quiet and peaceable life in all godliness and reverence. —1 Tim. 2:1,2

❦

Our pastors and leaders are gifts to the body of Christ and as a result serve on the frontlines of the battle of faith. Saturday night can be one of the toughest times on the frontlines for a pastor. Any night before he feeds the sheep can be stressful. Why?

Because the pastor's number one enemy targets him for distractions. A pastor friend said, "If I was an enemy to pastors, I would do my best to keep them confused, distracted, in debt and in pain in their life and especially before any message delivering the word of God. For I know and the devil knows all it takes is one word from God to change a life."

With that in mind, are you diligent to pray for our men and women of God called as leaders? They need your prayerful attention on a consistent basis. We encourage you to pray according to God's word, always. We offer no formulas just suggestions and tips to pray. Here are eight practical prayer suggestions to pray over your authority:

1. **Pray the Prayer of Agreement.**

Do you know your pastor's vision for your church? Has he or she started a new building program? Or has he launched a campaign to reach the youth in your area? Every leader needs the agreement of its followers. If not already, find out the specific vision of your house and pray the prayer of agreement. (Matt. 18:19)

2. Pray the Prayer of Safety.

We live in a dangerous violent world. Yet God watches over his Word to perform it. Pray that your leader(s) dwell in the secret place of the Most High and they remain stable and fixed under the shadow of the Almighty whose power no enemy can withstand. Thank God for the angels that he has given special charge over our leaders to accompany, defend and preserve in all their ways of obedience and service. (Isa. 26:3, Psa. 91)

3. Pray the Prayer of Peace.

Pray that God grants your leader peace that surpasses all understanding in mind, body and spirit. Pray that God grants him a peaceful dwelling place. Because we live in a fallen world, we may not always be able to enjoy a peaceful environment. But God can give us peace in the midst of a storm. Pray the prayer of peace for your authority. (Col. 3:15)

4. Pray the Prayer of healing.

Jesus paid a horrible price through his death, burial and resurrection that we might have life abundantly. Won't you pray that your leader receives healing whenever needed? Pray that he prosper, stay in good health even as his soul prospers. (3 John 2)

5. Pray the Prayer of Wisdom & Revelation.

Pray that the Spirit of the Lord will rest upon our authorities through the spirit of wisdom and understanding, the spirit of counsel and might, the spirit of knowledge. Ask that God will fill your leader with the knowledge of his will in all wisdom and spiritual understanding. (Isaiah. 11:2; Colossians. 1:9-13)

6. Pray the Prayer of Family Blessing.

Sometimes, if the enemy can't get to the man or woman of God he will target their family members. Pray that God grants them the joy of having every member of their families saved and healthy. Ask that their family life be blessed with special love and harmony.

7.   Pray the Prayer of Intercession.

Thank Father God for Jesus who ever lives to make intercession for us. But many times in our human thinking we don't know what we should pray. Don't forget to periodically ask the Holy Spirit to show you what to pray over your leader. Then faithfully, stand in the gap for your pastor that he may continue to walk victoriously in every area. (Heb 7:25)

8.   Pray the Prayer of Financial Blessing.

Pray that God would prosper them and give them health and bless them financially. Ask God to give them helpers who are full of the Spirit of wisdom to whom they can safely delegate the detailed duties and free them up to give themselves to prayer and the ministry of the Word.

It's hard to imagine the darkness that won't be held back if we don't pray or the good that will not come because we haven't prayed. The list above is not a comprehensive list of prayers. We have only scratched the surface with what can and should be prayed over our leaders. Join us as we become doers of this word of prayer and not just hearers by praying more for our pastors, leaders and those in authority over us.

Suggested Prayer: Lord, I thank you for our pastor (s), elders and other church leaders whom you have placed in the local body to keep us from being tossed to and fro, and carried about with every wind of doctrine...

Bless our leaders, Lord that they might govern your church according to your will. Help them be shepherds who never scatter the sheep, but who care for the flock, who watch for their souls, and seek those who are lost and troubled. Help me to be a support to them, to be available when they need me, to be always willing to help them and pray for them.

As Aaron and Hur upheld the arms of Moses in the heat of the battle, so may we ever uphold the arms of those you have appointed to lead us. Amen. (Excerpt from Prayers that Prevail, Victory House Publishers, Tulsa, OK)

Memory Principle: Serve making your life worthwhile

~~~~~~

The man who is born with a talent which he was meant to use finds his greatest happiness in using it. —Unknown

But life is worth nothing unless I use it for doing the work assigned to me by the Lord Jesus. —Acts 20:24a

CHAPTER SEVENTEEN

8 Highly Practical Ways to SERVE as Leader

Let this mind be in you which was also in Christ Jesus, who being in the form of God, did not consider it robbery to be equal with God, but made himself of no reputation, taking the form of a bond servant and coming in the likeness of men. —Phil. 2:5-7

☙

Did you lose sight of servant hood when you became a leader? Many leaders lose the correct view of serving once they are promoted to leadership. They lose sight of our chief example Jesus. He not counting himself equal with God took on the very nature of a servant. (Phil. 2:7) How much more should we as leaders in the Body of Christ do the same? Servant hood is an attitude in which each leader should seek to continue.

To cultivate the spirit of servanthood in your leadership, do these 8 practical things more and more:

1. Lead by Example.

Little children emulate their parents and big brothers and sisters in a family. In the same way, the little children of God do what they see their spiritual fathers, mothers, brothers and sisters do. Stay aware that you have little children in the faith watching what you do. Train them up right.

Let them see you serving your spouse or your immediate family. Be careful to allow them to see you giving in the offerings and engaging in worship. Before you know it you will have a whole flock of the children of God following you as you follow Christ because God can trust you to lead by example. (1 Cor. 11:1)

2. Lead in Obedience.

Continue to grow in your character through obedience to God. None of us have arrived so we must continue to work with God; growing in our character as the Holy Spirit leads. If there's something about yourself you don't like and you know you need to change, commit to change.

Perhaps you still struggle with a temper, selfishness or even bouts of pride. Practice what you preach allow the Holy Spirit to work on you. Be a living epistle (consistently changing and evolving for the better) not a history book. (2 Cor. 3:2,3)

3. Lead through Mentorship.

I encourage you to be open to mentorship. As leaders, Father God will send his dear ones to learn from you. Take another look at the one that's somehow always around—copying what you do. The Holy Spirit may be prompting you to impart to them.

Take a little extra time and talk to them. Find out where they want to go in God. It may be somewhere you've been and God wants YOU to show them the way or at least point the way.

4. Lead as Jesus Did.

Jesus humbled himself and took on the nature of a servant. Remember how the Apostle John described in detail the Last Supper where Jesus took off his outer garments and wrapped the servant's towel around his waist.

He took the water basin and knelt before the nearest disciple to wash his feet. He washed all of the disciples' feet; then standing up he charged them with following his example.

The Spirit of Servanthood Inspires Obedience

Many have written wanting to know how to gain more of a spirit of serving in their ministry, department or group. First of all, I want you to know Earma and I believe God has commissioned us to GO feed His sheep. In response to that call, we have been conducting Armorbearer and Ministry of Helps workshops whereby we teach and impart the spirit of armorbearing.

Furthermore, I encourage you to lead by example. From experience, many times we want those who follow us as we follow Christ to just-do-what-we-say. When it's a known fact that most of us do more of what we see. If you want more of an attitude of service among your ministry staff, volunteers and others commit to do these things:

Serve More. Start with your family. Surprise them; look for opportunities to serve them in ways you haven't before. For example, you've come home tired from a long day...go the extra mile find something undone and offer to do it. What does this have to do with your staff and volunteers? You'll see. As you serve more the spirit of serving will flow from your home to everything you do and beyond.

Check your obedience. Do you want the spirit of obedience to run rampant among your ranks? Whether it's our children, our staff or volunteers, we all desire to see more of the spirit of obedience in those we lead, right. Then check your obedience. Have you obeyed God in all known areas? Have you followed through in the last thing assigned to you by your chain of authority or mentor? If not, ask God for a fresh spirit of obedience in your life. Get ready to see a God ordained difference.

Commit to faithfulness. Your commitment to faithfulness will be modeled by everyone you influence. God called Abraham faithful by what he continued to do as well as what he believed. He finally said about him, "I know him (Abraham); he is faithful. He will teach his children and all those with him how to be faithful.

In His Service,
Varn Brown

5. Lead by Protecting the 3 Gs.

The three Gs are gentleness, graciousness and generosity. To protect these qualities in your life, you must stay sensitive to the Holy Spirit. He will help you cultivate a gentle spirit, maintain a gracious (kind) attitude and operate in a giving spirit. If you don't protect these Christ-like qualities you might find yourself wanting to beat the sheep in line or bang them over the head to get them to do what you need them to do.

6. Lead through your Authority Chain.

As a good leader you have setup your authority chain, delegating where you see fit. Now, after you've delegated, do your best to allow your delegated authority to operate in their given measure of rule. I mean don't interfere. Impart to, train and even guide your leaders but let them rule.

7. Lead as an Ambassador.

Recognize you are an Ambassador of our Lord. Increase as a gracious representative of Christ. Pray for and allow God's kindness and gentleness, his compassion to flow anew through you.

8. Lead while Guarding your Heart.

Guard your heart against offense, un-forgiveness and pride. Remember out of your heart flows the issues of life. If we allow un-forgiveness or pride to stay in our heart, it will open the door for other sins. Furthermore, Father God holds leaders to a higher standard; for the issues flowing from their heart affect so many more people.

God is raising up leaders and supporters in His Church. Put the above 8 tips above into practice: Lead more and more by example, in obedience, through mentorship, by doing what Jesus did, by protecting the 3 Gs, through your authority chain, as an ambassador and guarding your heart. Last but not least, while you are growing a great leadership team, remember to continue leading in the spirit of servanthood.

Memory Principle: Serve with Sense of Urgency

~~~~~~

When one door closes, another opens. Seize the opportunity while the path remains lit. —Unknown

As long as it is day, we must do the work of him who sent me. Night is coming, when no one can work. —*John 9:4*

CHAPTER EIGHTEEN

8 Highly Practical Ways to Appreciate Your Pastor

...In everything give thanks: for this is the will of God in Christ Jesus for you.
—1 Thessalonians 5:18

☞

Gratefulness is a diminishing force in our world. Even good manners, politeness seem to be in short supply. We often live at such a fast pace its easy to lose sight of what we are grateful for. Unthankfulness, rudeness and disrespect rule, if we allow it. Even so, it shouldn't be that way with God's people. We are called to be the light in a dark world. (Mt. 5:16) It honors God and glorifies him when we cultivate grateful hearts in our every day living. (1 Th. 5:18)

In fact, it's our responsibility to teach the next generation gratefulness. One good way we teach them gratefulness is by letting others know through our words and actions how they have benefited our lives. As with most life lessons, showing is much more effective than telling. The next generation must learn to appreciate others by watching it in action in our lives.

Appreciation has two primary meanings. One is to be thankful and the other is to increase in value. Have you examined what your behavior is teaching those around you about thankfulness and appreciation, lately? Are you teaching them to increasingly value our leadership? Moms, Dads are you teaching thankfulness by acting grateful toward each other.

Leaders are we teaching gratefulness for our government by praying for them? Or are we doing more pointing the finger than praying? Wherever you are in cultivating a grateful heart, won't you join us as we explore ways to show appreciation to our local church authorities? Here are some practical tips to teach gratefulness by appreciating our leaders.

1. **Send Thank You Card/Letter.**

   Politeness and good manners is a lost art in our society. If I took a poll, how many could say I sent a thank you card to appreciate someone for a kind deed. A good friend of mine said, "It was six months after the fact. I kept forgetting and finally didn't send it because it was too long."

   According to the late Ann Landers you can still send a thank you card up to a year. Any longer than that, the giver probably won't remember they gave you anything. So if nothing else, send your pastor a thank you card for a job well done this year. In other words, later is better than never but now is best.

2. **Plan a Pastor Appreciation Day.**

   Make it special. Make it a celebration. Plan a program for the day and invite pastor's friends or ask for video messages from closest friends. Present or send bouquet of flowers or balloons. It's a perfect time to include history review of ministry in the program. Add personal touches of member testimonials. You know what to do. Make it the best Pastor Appreciation Day ever.

3. **Throw a Food Festival in their Honor.**

   Invite the community. Theme the festival around their favorite ethnicity of food. Or mix it up and provide several kinds: Mexican, Italian, French, Asian, American, etc.

   Of course, a food festival is not a festival without music. Get the choir involved. Build a special choir for the festival day. According to the size of your congregation, enlist members to be a part of this special 100/1000 voice choir.

4. **Present a Plaque with Words of Appreciation.**

   Framed words are inspiring too. Most people enjoy mementos

that they can display in their home. Whatever you present, make it worthy. Treat it as an investment. I can hear someone saying, "I can't afford an investment."

That's all right; ask for the help of your brothers and sisters in Christ. Don't try to appreciate your leadership alone. Make it something they will be happy to showcase in their home for years to come. In other words, it's not in good taste to honor someone with something of poor quality.

5. **Meet a Need.**

Find out what their greatest need is at this time. Perhaps one of their appliances recently went out. Maybe pastor has been struggling to keep an old clunker going to get their family around. Invest in a better vehicle for them. Or a health challenge may have come up to take their extra cash. Study to be one of God's miracle workers in their life by meeting a need with no strings attached.

Remember if what you-plus-members have come up with does not quite cover it; give what you have toward it. God may have gotten them just to the point where you pick it up or he may use someone else to make up the difference.

6. **Fulfill a Desire.**

Find out their greatest desire and fulfill it. Perhaps they have been dreaming of taking a week long vacation. Travel agents can hunt down really great deals these days. Have you considered a new suit of clothing for Pastor(s)?

Again, think of it as an investment; buy the suit in completion with all accessories. Does your pastor own a really great family portrait or Pastor and spouse portrait? Commission an in-house artist or photographer to do their portrait. Commission it for their home or to showcase in the church.

7. **Send Flowers.**

Think of it this way. Give flowers to the living to appreciate them and not only to honor the dead. It doesn't just have to be for female pastors, either. Buy an arrangement for the pulpit in their honor.

Place a beautiful floral arrangement in your pastor's green room/ pre-service area.

If you send flowers make it an investment too. Buy at least 12-24 flowers. Its poor taste to send a puny bouquet of flowers. You may say, "But, what if 6 flowers are all I can afford?" Then our gentle suggestion would be to choose another appreciation method. There's lots of ways to appreciate your pastor, right?

8. **Send a Gift Basket.**

Fill it with things they enjoy. Cologne, perfume, lotions, candles and other personal care items make great gift baskets. Commission your favorite gift basket preparer or have some fun and fill it yourself with your pastor's favorite items.

Bath & Body Works and other similar stores are known for affordable great personal care gift baskets. Food gift baskets also make great gifts. Cookie baskets, fruit baskets, picnic baskets all sound good.

To sum it all up, don't forget to say *thank you*. Sometimes we miss the simplest form of blessing our pastor. Especially if you haven't done it in awhile remember to go verbally say thank you after one of his/her sermons.

Let them know how much you appreciate their efforts. If one of your pastor's recent sermons really impacted your life; now is the time to tell them. In honor of all the pastors and leaders reading this: May God's richest blessings rest upon you, your family and ministry.

Memory Principle: Serve with the lid off

~~~~~~

We've removed the ceiling above our dreams. There are no more impossible dreams. —Jesse Jackson

Everything is possible for him who believes. —*Mark 9:23b.*

How to Organize an Armorbearer Team in Your Local Church

Obey those that have authority over you so that it may go well with you.
—Hebrews 13:17

ভ

This is a model only so that you may personalize or tailor it to your specific armor bearer's team and duties. I have included a sample:

1. mission statement

2. general requirements

3. general duties

4. ministry dress code

5. qualifications of an Armorbearer

6. one year commitment statement

Include your church's (house vision) so that you may see it and run together. Whether you put it at the end or in front of your material, make sure all Armorbearers have read your church's overall vision. You will be structuring your team around what God has called your pastor and Church Body to do, right.

1. Mission Statement

To serve and support our leader(s) as (we) fulfill the vision of _____
_____ Church.

2. General Requirements:

• Understand God's delegated authority

• Commit to the vision of _____Church

• Work faithfully in the mission of _____ armorbearer's team

• Serve motivated by the heart of a servant (no hidden agendas)

3. General Duties:

• Assist pastors and leaders as assigned

• Shield pastors and leaders as needed

• Protect Shepherd's Lounge (green room)

• Create (prayerfully) a restful atmosphere in Shepherd's Lounge

• Provide refreshments (drinks, food, etc.) at/or between services

• Serve ministry guests

• Provide escort for ministry guest and family into church service

• Provide personal pickup for ministry guest (airport, hotel)

• Serve at special ministry functions (women and men)

• Enlist prayer warriors

4. Ministry Dress Code

Proper dress lets others know that you take your position, seriously. Also, our leaders will more readily recognize and treat you as a fellow minister if you look like one. Be neat, clean, and well-groomed. Dress modestly. (Some teams wear uniforms) Avoid clothing short or tight. Please conform to the following standard of dress while serving.

Women

• Nice dress

• Modestly fit

Men

• Sunday best clothing

• Nice slacks and clean shirt

• Properly shaven

• Polished shoes

Both

• Clean and neat hair

• Clean hands and body

• Breath mints

5. Qualifications of an Armorbearer In Local Church

1. Be a member of Church for at least one year.

2. Attend the Armorbearer's class or small group study.

3. Complete the volunteer request form.

4. Be an (already) active and consistent participator in volunteer ministry.

5. Supply two references (i.e., ministry leader, elder, or pastor)

6. Write a short explanation letter answering the question: Why do you want to be an Armorbearer for _____ church?

7. Commit to volunteer a minimum of one year in this position.

6. One Year Commitment Statement:

As an Armorbearer of _____Church, I understand my responsibilities are:

• *To maintain proper priorities and balance in my life and family "God, spouse, children, work and _____ Church."*
• *To assist Pastors and their pastoral team in implementing the vision the Lord has given them for the ministry at _____Church.*
• *To work as a team in fulfilling the vision and mission of Armorbearers at _____Church.*

Everything I do relating to the work of this ministry will be done with the spirit of excellence and as unto the Lord. I realize as an armorbearer in _____ Church that demands will be made upon my time. I will endeavor to increase the amount of time with the Lord in prayer and study of the Word.

I will seek to stay in tune with the Holy Spirit so that I may continue serving motivated by the heart of a servant. I realize that staying in tune with the Holy Spirit will help me be an anticipator of the needs of our leaders.

Because I, also, understand that developing relationships within the team and with our leaders take time, I will commit to serve as an Armorbearer in Church throughout the entire calendar year.

I realize that if I have a life status change or the Lord clearly directs me into another area of ministry, I will be released from the one year commitment as an armorbearer at _____ Church.

Signed _____
Date _____

Notes

ભ

Notes for original book *In the Spirit of Armorbearing* and *In the Spirit of Armorbearing Small Group Study Edition*

Chapter One: What is an Armorbearer?

1. See 1 Samuel 16.
2. See Ephesians 6.
3. James Strong, Strong's Complete Dictionary of Bible Words (Thomas Nelson Publishers, 1996), help (#5375).
4. See 1 Timothy 1:18; 6:12.
5. See Exodus 17:11, 12.
6. See II Kings.
7. See I Samuel 16, 17.
8. Michael Agnes and Charlton Laird, eds., Webster's New World Dictionary and Thesaurus, Compilation Staff of Webster's New World Dictionary (Simon and Schuster, Inc., 1996), serve, p. 566.
9. Webster's, refresh, p. 520.
10. See Ecclesiastes 1:9, 10.
11. See 1 Samuel 16.

Chapter Two: Fulfilling Your High Calling to Ministry

1. Tommy Tenney, God's Secrets to Greatness (Ventura: Regal Books, 2000), p.48.
2. See 1 Corinthians 12:20, 22.
3. See I Kings 19:19-21.
4. See John 15:16.

5. See Revelation 17:14.

6. See 1 Corinthians 12:28.

7. John 15:16.

8. I Samuel 30:24.

9. See 1 Corinthians 12:27, 28.

10. See 1 Corinthians 12:18.

11. See Acts 6.

12. See 2 Peter 1:2-10.

13. See Romans 12:6,7 AMP

14. See Daniel 1:20.

15. See Ephesians 1:17.

16. Flegal KM, Carroll MD, Kuczmarski RJ, Johnson CL. Overweight and Obesity in the United States: Prevalence and Trends, 1960-1994. Int J Obes. 1998;22:39-47.

17. See Romans 5:3, 4 (The Living Bible, Tyndale House Publishers, Inc., 1971).

18. See 1 Peter 1:14.

19. See Romans 12:10.

20. See 1 Peter 2:17.

21. See Ephesians 6:18.

22. See 1 John 3:18.

23. See 2 Timothy 2:21 (The Living Bible, Tyndale House Publishers, Inc., 1971).

24. See 2 Peter 1:2-10.

Chapter Three: Anointed to Serve

1. See Acts 6:1-6.

2. See John 14:15-21.

3. See James 3:13-17.

4. See Romans 11:29.

5. See Matthew 25:14-30.

6. See Revelation 3:15, 16.

7. See 1 Peter 1:16.

8. Kenneth E. Hagin, Sr., I Believe in Visions (Tulsa: RHEMA Bible Church, 1984), p. 57.

9. See 1 Corinthians 9:27.

10. See 1 Corinthians 13:1-13.

11. See Jeremiah 33:3.

Chapter Four: Choosing God's View of Servanthood

1. See Philippians 2:7.

2. See Ephesians 6:7.

3. See 1 Chronicles 9:17-33.

4. See 1 Chronicles 9:20

5. See 1 Chronicles 9:22.

6. See 1 Chronicles 9:23 TLB.

7. See 1 Chronicles 9:29 TLB.

8. See 1 Chronicles 9:33,34 TLB paraphrased.

9. See James 1:27.

10. See Hebrews 12:2.

11. See 1 Corinthians 10:31b

Chapter Five: Understanding the Flow of Authority

1. See Ephesians 6:12.

2. See Romans 13:2.

3. See Matthew 8:5-13.

4. Earma Broadway Brown, Broken Church Recovery (Dallas: Butterfly Press, 1997).

5. See Ephesians 5:20.

6. See Hebrews 13:17.

7. See 1 Peter 5:5a paraphrased.

8. See Acts 9:16 AMP

9. 1 Timothy 2:1, 2.

10. See Luke 2:41-52 paraphrased.

Chapter Six: Being the Gift of Support

1. See 1 Peter 4:10-11.

2. See Numbers 18:6.

3. See 1 Corinthians 12:18.

4. See 1 Peter 1:16.

5. See Luke 11:13 paraphrased.

6. See Exodus 4:14-17.

7. See Exodus 17:11-12.

8. See 1 Peter 4:13

9. See 1 Corinthians 12:12-21.

10. See Exodus 6:20; 7:1-2; 14; 17:1-7; 18; Deuteronomy 1:9-18;
Leviticus 8-9; Exodus 17:8-16.

Chapter Seven: Developing the Spirit of Armorbearing

1. See Jeremiah 36; 43.

2. See 1 Corinthians 12:18.

3. 1 Peter 3:8.

4. John 15:13.

5. See Matthew 20:1-16.

6. John 9:4.

7. See John 15:13.

8. See Proverbs 18:12.

9. See 1 Thessalonians 5:12, 13.

10. See 2 Timothy 3:12.

11. See John 15:18a, 20a.

12. See John 15:19.

13. See Exodus 16:2; 86:9.

14. See Hebrews 6:1a.

15. See II Kings 3:11-27.

Chapter Nine: From the Heart of an Armorbearer

1. See Numbers 16-18.

2. See 1 Samuel 14.

3. See Exodus 17:11-12.

4. See John 15:16.

5. See Exodus 31:1, 6.

6. John C. Maxwell, 21 Irrefutable Laws of Leadership (Nashville:
Thomas Nelson Publishers, 1998), p. 90.

7. See 2 Corinthians 13:1.

8. See 1 Peter 5:5.

9. See John 15:20.

10. See Psalms 62:1, 2.

11. See John 15:13.

12. T.D. Jakes, Keepers of the Flame, 4-tape audio series, tape 4 (Dallas: T.D. Jakes Ministries, 2000).

13. See Mark 14:38.

14. See 1 Samuel 14.

Chapter Ten: The Ministry of an Armorbearer

1. See Matthew 10:41

2. See Exodus 31:1-11; Hebrews 8:2.

3. See 1 Timothy 2:2

4. See 1 Chronicles 12:1-40.

5. See Judges 7:8.

6. See John 9:4.

7. Matthew 25:45-51

8. 1 Corinthian 13.

9. 1 Chronicles 12.

Chapter Eleven: Developing the Character of Christ

1. See Deuteronomy 8:4.

2. See Hebrews 12:11.

3. See Deuteronomy 8:2, 3.

4. See Romans 5:4, 5.

5. John Maxwell, The 21 Indispensable Qualities of a Leader (Nashville: Thomas Nelson Publishers, 1999), p. 4.

6. See I Samuel 3.

7. See 1 Chronicles 12:22.

8. See 2 Timothy 2:3.

9. See 1 John 1:9, Romans 8:28

Chapter Twelve: Becoming an Anticipator

1. See James 1:5.

2. See Isaiah 65:24a.

3. See John 12:1-8.

4. See Matthew 10:39.

5. See Matthew 7:14.

6. See Psalms 33:1.

7. See Proverbs 22:3; 27:12.

Chapter Thirteen: The Gehazi Factor

1. See 1 Corinthians 10:6.

2. See 2 Kings 5:20-27.

3. See 1 Peter 5:6.

4. See Galatians 5:16-26.

5. See 1 Peter 5:8

Chapter Fourteen: Daring to Be Faithful

1. See Romans 5:20.

2. Buddy Bell, The Ministry of Helps Handbook (Tulsa, OK: Harrison House, Inc., 1990), p. 20.

3. See Genesis 18:19 TLB; James 2:21-26; 5:17 TLB paraphrased.

4. Hebrews 6:10.

5. See Romans 12:1.

6. See Hebrews 12:11.

7. See Psalms 91:4.

8. See 1 Corinthians 4:1, 2.

9. See Matthew 18:19.

10. See Joshua 24.

11. See John 18:15-27; 21:15-23.

About the Author

Varn and Earma Brown, author and ministers of the gospel live in northern Texas. Former armorbearers and ministry assistants to their Senior Pastors Mike and Kathy Hayes at Covenant Church, the Brown's passion and anointing in serving their local church and community is contagious to people in a wonderful way.

For participation in your conferences, speaking engagements and armorbearer workshops contact speaking@armorbearers.net or call *Armorbearers International* at **877-714-1756.**

Quick Order Form

🏷 **Email orders:** orders@armorbearers.net

🖨 **Fax orders:** (877) 714-1756. Send this form.

☎ **Telephone orders:** Call (877) 714-1756

🗐 **Postal Orders:** P.O. Box 1114, Wylie, TX 75098

Please send the following books at $14.99.

Quantity (   ) _____

See our web site http://www.armorbearers.net for other resources and sign-up for updates & mailing lists.

Name: _____

Address: _____

City, State/Province, Postal Code:

_____

Tel: _____

Email: _____

Sales tax: _____

Shipping: _____

Payment: Check _____ Credit card: _____

Visa ( ) MasterCard ( ) Optima ( ) AMEX ( ) Discover ( )

Card number: _____

Name on card: _____

Exp. Date _____

CPSIA information can be obtained at www.ICGtesting.com
Printed in the USA
LVOW042344181012

303536LV00001B/112/P